M

Do I Have to Wear Black
to a Funeral?

Do I Have to Wear Black to a Funeral?

112 Etiquette Guidelines for the New Rules of Death

Florence Isaacs

THE COUNTRYMAN PRESS
A division of W. W. Norton & Company
Independent Publishers Since 1923

This book is intended as a general guide and does not substitute for legal or professional advice. Neither the publisher nor the author of this book guarantees its accuracy and completeness for all purposes. References to specific products, services, service providers and/or organizations are for illustration only and none should be read to suggest an endorsement or a guarantee of performance. As of press time, the URLs displayed in this book link or refer to existing websites. Neither the publisher nor the author is responsible for, and neither may be deemed to endorse or recommend, any website other than its or her own.

Copyright © 2020 by Florence Isaacs

All rights reserved
Printed in the United States of America

For information about permission to reproduce selections from this book, write to Permissions, The Countryman Press, 500 Fifth Avenue, New York, NY 10110

For information about special discounts for bulk purchases, please contact W. W. Norton Special Sales at specialsales@wwnorton.com or 800-233-4830

Manufacturing by Versa Press
Book design by Anna Reich
Production manager: Devon Zahn

Library of Congress Cataloging-in-Publication Data

Names: Isaacs, Florence, author.
Title: Do I have to wear black to a funeral : 112 etiquette guidelines for the new
    rules of death / Florence Isaacs.
Identifiers: LCCN 2019037678 | ISBN 9781682683569 (paperback) |
    ISBN 9781682683576 (epub)
Subjects: LCSH: Mourning etiquette—United States—Miscellanea. |
    Funeral rites and ceremonies—United States—Miscellanea.
Classification: LCC BJ2071 .I73 2020 | DDC 395.2/3—dc23
LC record available at https://lccn.loc.gov/2019037678

The Countryman Press
www.countrymanpress.com

A division of W. W. Norton & Company, Inc.
500 Fifth Avenue, New York, NY 10110
www.wwnorton.com

978-1-68268-356-9 (pbk.)

10 9 8 7 6 5 4 3 2 1

To Joshua, Zoe, and Dean

•CONTENTS•

•INTRODUCTION•

I've been writing about etiquette since 1995, when my first book *Just a Note to Say . . . The Perfect Words for Every Occasion* was published. I continued to do so with *My Deepest Sympathies . . . Meaningful Sentiments for Condolence Notes and Conversations, Plus a Guide to Eulogies* (2000). I subsequently became a blogger for Legacy.com, where I wrote the blogs *Sincere Condolences* and *Widow in the World*, leading the *New York Times* to dub me "the Dear Abby of death." Questions I received from readers opened my eyes to the unique issues both the bereaved and the rest of us face. This book reflects the types of questions I received, and the advice I dispensed, and covers new issues that are arising today.

Past generations dealt with death as a part of life, and communication was face-to-face or via the mail (the one without the *e* in front). But people rarely die at home today, and what used to be a family/community support system has given way to hospitals and hospice. Technology has turned some of the healing rituals surrounding death upside down. Causes of death have changed. People are living with AIDS, but dying of opioid addiction. Environmental issues have become factors in burials.

Furthermore, the revolution in technology has changed the way many of us communicate with each other when death occurs, whether the deceased is our own loved one or someone else's. It's not unusual for the bereaved to announce the death of a parent to their 100 closest "friends" on social media. How do you respond if you're a recipient? Do you push Like? Do you email a condolence message? Or do you rely on the advice your mother gave you and send an old-school handwritten condolence note by mail? Such questions didn't exist before the age of technology, and the rules keep changing. Who would have guessed thirty years ago that cremations would top traditional interments in our society or that cemeteries would run out of burial plots or that many parents and grandparents would live into their nineties or beyond. (An Ohio woman recently died at 114.) It's hard to know how to express sympathy, behave appropriately, and make sensible choices. What's right may vary, depending on who *you* are, the nature of your relationship with the bereaved, and the power dynamic between you. (For example, it's probably not appropriate to send that virtual hug to your boss.)

This book is a guide to navigating rules, practices, and traditions that are steadily evolving as our society grows more secular. The very definition of "bereaved" has shifted as well. There may be an inordinate number of people who qualify—or think they do. It's a challenge to compile a list of survivors for the obituary of someone who was married multiple times (and who is the parent or stepparent of many). Some families mention the dog in the obituary and omit stepsiblings.

According to the latest data available, about 2,800,000 people die in the United States each year. That generates a lot of funerals and memorial services, wakes and visitations, burials and cremations, and condolence messages. The number of annual deaths will only grow as the population continues to age.

This book will guide you through attending a funeral or memorial service (or planning one), extending condolences (or acknowledging them), and so much more with confidence. You'll learn about the trend to personalization, which focuses on ways to reflect who the deceased really was. Whole new categories of funeral and death workers have emerged to accommodate these changes, as well. Ever hear of a death doula or a funeral celebrant? In this age of high anxiety, you'll learn how to deftly handle the newest situations.

Death is the great equalizer. It's going to happen to everyone—those we love and don't, the smart and less smart, zillionaires and the rest of us. This book gives you a grip on responding to a death as a bereaved, a bystander, a colleague or coworker, a contact or client, a friend, a neighbor, or an in-law. My goal is to offer you honest information on how to proceed even if the bereaved practice an unfamiliar religion or have opted for a ritual you're attending for the first time, like a humanist ceremony or a green funeral. I promise to provide fresh insights on what's appropriate to say and do, even in the most heartbreaking situations. For example, the right words for one person can actually anger someone else, depending on age, tech expertise, and a host of other variables. But relax. I present strategies to guide you through the thicket in these changing times. My goal is to cut through the confusion. After all, what's more unsettling than death, which can be drenched in pain, mystery, despair, and loss, sometimes all at the same time?

You'll also learn how to cope when you are the bereaved. What do you do when your parent suddenly dies of a heart attack—and you're abruptly in charge of everything? And are you aware that your own end-of-life planning is a great gift to those who care about you, not to mention yourself? Read on for answers to the most frequently asked questions about death, dying, and memorializing.

When Someone Else's
Loved One Dies

Death and its rituals and ramifications are hot topics these days. Obituaries are typically second only to the front page as the most-read section of newspapers, and the trend is growing, according to the National Newspaper Association. Many people visit cemeteries when they travel—I personally love visiting historical and unusual cemeteries because they tell so many stories. I am touched when I come across the weathered stone grave marker of a toddler who died of diphtheria, a disease that was a killer in its time. Civil War cemeteries fascinate me. The soldiers were so young. Other fascinating examples include the graveyard at Long Branch Baptist Church in Dalzell, South Carolina, which holds the dead of Turkish descent who emigrated from the Middle East and are believed to have helped in the fight against the British in the Revolutionary War. I love seeing New Orleans cemeteries, where bodies are buried above ground. At the St. Louis #1

Cemetery, which dates back to 1789, you'll find the grave of a voodoo queen among other spooky attractions.

While wandering through cemeteries, I sometimes stumble upon a celebrity's grave. I was recently in Louisville, Kentucky, where Muhammad Ali lies in Cave Hill Cemetery. This is one of the most beautiful cemeteries I've seen, and it features many gorgeous stone monuments. Ali's gravestone bears the inscription, "Service to others is the rent you pay for your room in heaven." African American Cemetery No. 2 in Lexington, Kentucky, is on the National Register of Historic Places. Among those buried here are the first jockey to win the Kentucky Derby and our nation's first African American postmaster.

According to the International Southern Cemetery Gravestone Association, people used to bury deceased family members in plots near their homes before there were cemeteries. Out of concern that the dead would rise, they piled stones, rocks, and wood on the grave.

Gravestones can be traced back to even earlier times. Their use comes from a Jewish custom that honors the deceased by the placing of stones at the head of the grave. Stones (unlike flowers, which fade and die) represent a lasting memorial.

For all of this historical interest, most people find it hard to deal with death in the present. Let's face it: Death scares us, well, to death. And today we confront the specter of sudden death and assaults on our sense of safety in the form of out-of-the-blue massacres at schools, concerts, restaurants, and places of employment. These kinds of unimaginable losses seem to have become part of the cultural landscape.

Whether an expected death has occurred, or an unimaginable tragedy causes a death, it's important to behave well and show respect and concern, even when you feel at a loss for what to do or say. If you are paying respects to the bereaved, you may face a thicket of relationships to sort out. You may have to navigate multiple marriages or alliances, stepchildren and parents, and even people who consider themselves "just like a daughter." At the same time, respected rules surrounding a death may no longer apply. In terms of etiquette, it can be a minefield. Let's dive in.

1.

Should I call (or call on) the bereaved as soon as I hear of a death?

In some communities, phone calls and visits immediately after a death are customary expressions of support. Everyone rallies round. However, there can be a thin line between support and intrusion. Calling can also be a mistake if the bereaved are not close to you, especially if the death is unexpected. When a loved one dies out of the blue, the family may well be in shock and barely able to function. They may not wish to talk to casual acquaintances at this time. When in doubt, one thing is certain: You can't go wrong with a condolence note or card.

For example, a couple who lost a teenaged child hated such calls and wanted to be left alone, except for their nearest and dearest. Yet people with the best of intentions called daily. One relationship blew up as a result. The bereaved felt assaulted. The callers felt unappreciated.

It can be tricky to navigate such circumstances. Due to technology, we are living through an extraordinary upheaval in social mores surrounding deaths. Today, you can accomplish an ongoing connection by writing or emailing instead of calling, as in "Just checking in to say 'Hi.' You don't have to answer this." Texting is more immediate, but I wouldn't use it unless you are very close to the bereaved. It can backfire and feel like an imposition.

2. How should I spread the word about a death to others who know the person?

If the deceased is a relative, friend, or coworker, then the job is simple. Both of you know the deceased. I'd get to the point directly right away with something like, "I have bad news. Gregory has died." The expected communication about details—online or in person—will automatically ensue. But follow the lead of the family. Do not post about a death until the bereaved have announced it online. Would you want your aunt to find out your mother has died from strangers on Facebook?

3. Where can I find information about funeral details? I have learned someone has died and I wish to attend, if possible.

They will probably be included in the obituary, if there is one. If you haven't seen the obituary or don't know if one exists, you can look it up on Legacy.com or similar sites. You can also ask friends or family of the deceased for information about the funeral. If you know the name of the funeral home (if one is involved), you can call and request the details about funeral time, whether the family will receive people before or after the service, and other guidance. The obituary or funeral home will provide information such as the date and time of service, whether the burial will take place after the funeral, and where.

If information isn't included in the obituary, the funeral is probably private—in other words, it is limited to family and others who have already been notified. Why does the family make this decision? It may be due to limited finances. Or the family may want privacy. Or the deceased may have made the decision beforehand. Regardless, this is a time to respect the family's (or deceased's) wishes and stay home. You certainly can, however, send a condolence note or card. In rare cases, a private funeral is also a way to bar unwelcome guests, such as an unstable ex-spouse or others. It's a lot easier to withhold the information from the public than it is to deal with calling in the police to eject someone unwanted.

4. I hate funerals, but I must go occasionally. How can I make the experience less of an ordeal?

First, understand that it isn't just you. Most of us feel uncomfortable about attending a funeral or memorial service because it's about death. We don't want to be reminded that it happens to all of us sooner or later—that nobody escapes. Someone else's death shatters our deep-down illusions that we're going to live forever. Yet there are ways to arrive prepared.

Whatever you do, don't show up "cold turkey," without giving a thought to what has happened, how you feel about it, and who you are likely to meet and talk to there. First, do your

homework and consider what you will say to the bereaved—
and why. This is very important because it's easy to get into
trouble. (See Question 21: "How do you find the right words
to express condolences?" on page 44.)

If you're attending the service alone, consider possible sce-
narios for engaging others who might be sitting or standing
next you. Make a list of possible "openers." Yes, it's hard for
many of us to start conversations with strangers. Yet it helps
build confidence to inquire, "How are you connected to the
bereaved (or the deceased)?" I've used this line many times and
find that people are more than happy (and even relieved) to
talk. Chances are, they feel as uncomfortable and anxious as
you do and will welcome the distraction. You can start some
fascinating conversations this way as you both share information and memories. Listen to the response and comment on
it, if appropriate, to encourage continuing the conversation. Or
add something like, "I went to high school with Joe." Or, "I was
a volunteer at a soup kitchen with Mary."

5. What's the difference between a funeral and a memorial service?

The body is present at a funeral. There is no body at a memorial service, either because the family prefers it that way (perhaps because the body is disfigured or emaciated after a long

illness) or because the remains were never found (as in war situations or some plane crashes). Another defining feature: The timing of a memorial service is flexible, which can be critical these days when families are often scattered all over the country (or the world). A memorial service can be held at any time as a convenience for far flung family members and friends. The obituary may say, "A private memorial service will be held at a later date." Or the wording may specify the service will be held in a given month. There may be more than one service in different localities to accommodate friends and relatives.

A memorial service might also be more casual than a funeral and might be held in a hotel or other space. It is more likely to be a "celebration of life." For example, a memorial service for a cabaret singer included films of some of her performances, and left attendees teary-eyed.

6. When is attending a funeral or memorial service "a must"—and when is it optional?

Sometimes the decision is clear-cut, but not always. It helps to ask yourself, "What are good and sufficient reasons to attend?" For example, some of us do ourselves a disservice by staying home. Showing up can provide big benefits for our emotional health and our souls. Funerals are never easy, but they are a time to think of the deceased's impact on us. The service can also help us reflect on ourselves and where we are in our own lives. They can tune us in to whether we may wish to make adjustments. These issues tend to get lost in our high-speed, constantly working world. Meaning is hard to find when we're glued to our cell phones. Funerals can be an opportunity to realize we're finite as we grapple with the idea of death—to reflect on what it means to have this one life and how to live it.

Online funerals and condolences, and exchanges on social media, remove us from the reality of death. What's lost is tangible community and solace. The bereaved appreciate our physical presence. It's important for them to contemplate the death of a loved one together with others who care.

On the other hand, health, finances, and other issues can get in the way. How far you're going to extend yourself depends on your relationship with the bereaved and/or the deceased. Attendance is totally up to you if your connection is a casual one. You can stay home and, if you wish, send a condolence note—or a sympathy card with a personal handwritten line or two (or not). It's different if a close friend or relative died or is in mourning. In that case, I would try my best to be there.

For example, I attended the funeral of a dear cousin who lived several states away. It was costly and inconvenient to make the trip, but he had been extremely kind and helpful to me on several occasions. A bonus was the opportunity to see other far-away family members who attended. On the other hand, some relatives stayed home. Each of us has a singular relationship with other family members and different limits on how much inconvenience is too much.

If your connection is business-related, it's usually safe to follow the lead of colleagues or coworkers. When everyone else is attending, it's smart to join them.

Ambivalent about attending or not? I'd ask myself, "What are acceptable reasons to skip this funeral?" My list would be (1) If you're sick. Headaches don't count unless they're migraines. A bout with the flu qualifies as a reason to forego the service, too, either because it's debilitating to you or because you may spread the misery to other attendees. In the case of a hacking cough, you don't want the noise to repeatedly interrupt services. (2) Really bad weather: a flood, hurricane, explosion, forest fire, mudslide, or your plane is grounded. If in doubt, check with others you trust for their opinions. (3) It conflicts with your vacation. This is a tricky excuse. But let's face the truth: Are you going to cancel your trip to Australia and lose big bucks on deposits and reservation changes? Probably not for a distant relative. But what if it's your beloved parent or sibling who has died? Ultimately, these decisions are personal.

It's worth mentioning that when my husband died, I noticed people at the funeral who I never expected to attend. They went the extra mile, and I never forgot it.

7. How long should I stay at a condolence call?

It depends on your relationship with the deceased or the bereaved. A very close friend in either case might stay an hour (or two or three) to just "be there" for the bereaved, as well as help with practical chores like greeting visitors and putting out food. A colleague at work might stay for twenty or thirty minutes.

8. Is it necessary to sign the funeral home register or an online register?

Consider it a courtesy and solace to the bereaved, who value your presence and want to know who has paid respects to them. Survivors also often read and reread the register over time and reminisce about those who have "shown up." Sign in even if you and the deceased were close friends and/or you know the family well. If your connection is entirely to the deceased, write an explanation of how you know him or her, as in, "We were hired on the same day at XYZ Corporation and became friends." It comforts the family to hear about such connections.

9. If nobody is talking about the cause of death, is it okay to ask about it?

Because it's a factual question, you may assume, "Why not ask?" There are times when the family may be comfortable with disclosure. In one case, for example, the answer was: The deceased died due to an undiagnosed cancer. The doctor messed up and missed it. However, there are times when the family may not want to disclose the cause of death because they feel a stigma of some sort is involved. They may not want to mention the death was due to suicide—or opioid overdose, for instance.

Be sensitive and ask someone other than the bereaved unless you are a close family friend or relative. The bereaved may not want to discuss the circumstances with the wider world. If I was an acquaintance, I would not raise the subject at all. Instead, I'd check the obituary, which may say something like, "(Deceased) died after a long battle with breast cancer" or "due to complications of pneumonia." Don't bother asking the funeral home, which is likely to protect the family's privacy.

10. What should I wear? Can I wear green to the funeral?

The Romans wore just plain black, without adornment of any kind. In parts of Portugal, Spain, Italy, Russia, and Greece, some widows may still wear black for the rest of their lives.

Every culture marks a death in its own way, although there are common threads that link us all. Buddhists, who believe in reincarnation, may wear white to encourage rebirth of the deceased. Confucian tradition is also to wear white while mourning. Queen Victoria wanted to be buried with her white wedding veil over her face. *Deuil blanc* or "white mourning" is a French term for wearing white for children and single women. In the Middle Ages, queens of Europe wore white, including for the deaths of in-laws, as in the case of Mary, Queen of Scots.

When sixty-two-year-old King Baudouin of Belgium died of a heart attack in Spain in 1993, his widow Queen Fabiola wore white.

Don't wear red, which signifies happiness, to a Chinese funeral. But red is fine in South Africa, where the color signifies the bloody history of apartheid. Purple may be a mourning color in Guatemala and Brazil, and it's worn by widows in Thailand. If a husband dies in Papua New Guinea, his widow wears gray.

In the Western world, black is the traditional color of mourning, but these days, you can generally wear green or virtually any color to most funerals or memorial services, especially if it's a "celebration of life." Although green does symbolize death in South America, the color is likelier to represent life and new birth elsewhere (as well as wealth and money). Use common sense, however. It's not about you, and the point is to blend in and show respect. For women, a flaming red blouse with a low neckline or a short skirt is usually unacceptable. You're attending to honor the deceased and pay your respects to the survivors, not to audition for a Broadway musical. For men, a beer T-shirt is appropriate at the local bar. It has no place at a memorial service. You can't go wrong with a jacket and tie— and you can always remove the jacket later if you wish.

If you're going to St. Patrick's Cathedral or a similar venue, wear a nice suit, shirt, and tie. That said, regional differences do count, as do weather conditions. People tend to dress more casually out West than on the East Coast. At a rancher's funeral in rural Utah, jeans and cowboy boots and hats may be the clothing of choice. Young pallbearers at one of the funerals for victims of the mass shooting at Marjory Stoneman Douglas High School in Parkland, Florida, wore short sleeved knit shirts and dark pants. It's hot down there.

Another variable is your connection to the deceased—the more casual the acquaintance the more casually you can be dressed, yet you want to fit in, and erring on the side of darker, more conservative clothing is safe. You can also ask yourself, "What do I tend to wear when I go to my place of worship?" You're paying respects and a funeral is usually a solemn occasion. If there's any doubt in your mind, call the funeral home or a family member in advance and ask.

On the other hand, some bereaved don't want all black at funerals and may ban black altogether. Families may choose colors to personalize a funeral and make it a celebration of life rather than a solemn occasion. Family members may consider color a tribute to the deceased who was full of life, energy, and fun. Examples abound. One deceased left instructions before she died that she wanted a party—and attendees dressed in any color but black. At a service in Oregon, everyone wore Hawaiian shirts to honor an uncle. To honor a deceased who was a sneaker collector, attendees at his funeral were asked to wear their favorite versions. One couple bought clean new Nikes for the occasion. At a funeral for a hat designer, some people shopped for and wore amazing hats as a tribute to her. At another service, some attendees wore polka dots and sang songs together.

The point is, funerals or memorial services are emotionally draining for everyone. Most of us dread going. If you're there to pay your respects, you'll feel a lot more comfortable if you don't have to worry about an inappropriate appearance. Ask yourself, "Is this an occasion to stand out from the crowd—or not?"

There are quieter ways of dressing as a tribute to the deceased. For example, at the public visitation preceding former First Lady Barbara Bush's funeral, many mothers and daughters wore white pearls (her signature while she lived at the White House) in her honor.

For specific guidance on the dress code for individual religious services, see Funeral Guide by Religion, page 69.

11. I've been asked to be a pallbearer at the funeral of a friend. I've never done it before and feel kind of anxious. What's expected of me? Also, can someone volunteer to be a pallbearer?

Caskets tend to weigh 100 to 300 pounds. Funeral homes use carriages to wheel caskets inside their facilities, so the only carrying of the casket is from the hearse into the place of service and out again to the hearse afterward for the trip to the cemetery and the grave. Men should usually dress in a suit and tie, but double check with the funeral home, especially if the weather is threatening. Make a checklist to be prepared and avoid missteps. Ask the funeral home or family about the time schedule so that you arrive with time to spare. (You may be expected to be there earlier than ordinary attendees.) Act responsibly and listen carefully to instructions and directions.

As for volunteering, I wouldn't advise it. It can put the bereaved in an awkward position at a time when they're already stretched to the limit. (Nobody likes to say, "No. We've already chosen pallbearers.") On the other hand, it's an honor to be asked to be a pallbearer and it's bad form to refuse (unless you have a solid excuse, such as you're having surgery or you must attend another funeral across the country that day).

12. Why don't we see women pallbearers?

Well . . . we do, but they're rare. For example, Maria Shriver was a pallbearer at the funeral of her mother, Eunice Kennedy Shriver, sister of President Kennedy and the founder of the Special Olympics. Practicalities are involved, such as the casket weight, which is likely to be a stretch for many women, although it may be doable if shared with other pallbearers.

At a recent funeral in Ghana, all the pallbearers were women, who even danced around with the coffin, despite the heavy load. Weight can even be a challenge for some men: A man in Indonesia was crushed to death at his mother's funeral when her coffin slipped the grip of pallbearers ascending a funeral tower.

Women pallbearers also need to forget about fashion and wear comfortable shoes and clothing, especially if the weather is bad and the ground is muddy.

13. How about children and disabled people as pallbearers?

At Barbara Bush's funeral, her grandsons served as pallbearers and President George H. W. Bush followed the coffin in a wheelchair, pushed by his president son. In some cases children may follow the coffin.

14. What exactly is a eulogy?

The word derives from the Greek for "praise." When used at a funeral, a eulogy celebrates and explains the deceased's achievements and character. Such stories can be very powerful. However, a eulogy is also a mournful or melancholy poem or song, especially a funeral song or lament for the dead. The secret of a great eulogy is honesty and sincerity. Perhaps eulogies are especially popular today because we want someone to "sum up" a life, to give it meaning. (Usually, we're all so busy that we have no time to just sit around and share thoughts and feelings in the course of living our lives.)

15. I've been asked to give a eulogy for a close friend who was killed in a boating accident. I've never given one before. How should I proceed? What are the basics to follow?

The good news is eulogies should run no longer than five to seven minutes. Remember, you're summing up the highlights of someone's life, not writing a biography. And little details can bring smiles and tears, as in, "She was a history nut and loved accounts of the Civil War and World War II. But she had her secrets, too—romance novels. She said they relaxed her and believed that anyone who didn't read some trash was suspect."

What matters most is what you have to say, not how seamlessly you say it. Few of us are orators. You can start with a memory, as in, "John was four years younger than me and I loved him to pieces. He was quite simply adorable, always smiling, and had the family trait—dimples. In his high school years he became a football star in our little corner of the world, and eventually won a scholarship to Notre Dame. He went on to become a leader in education. He had enormous career success—along with personal tragedy." Humor is very welcome at funerals, so good-natured personal anecdotes, be it about his movie mania or his supplemental income from playing cards, would fit right in.

No one expects you to be Abraham Lincoln. Think of it as speaking privately to someone who knew the deceased. You don't have to be eloquent, but do try to be pithy. Nothing is worse than someone who drones on and on. I've actually seen a best man booed while giving an endless speech at a wedding. That wouldn't happen at a funeral, due to the occasion, but the audience might start booing internally.

16. Can a eulogy be funny?

Relax. Eulogies can absolutely be humorous, as long as they're also loving. Celebrations of the deceased are surely in vogue. After pop singer (and Republican congressman) Sonny Bono died in a skiing accident, his ex-wife Cher gave a eulogy where she spoke of him telling her he was descended from Napoleon. (She also made fun of herself for believing him.)

Humor works when the deceased had a great sense of humor and would have appreciated being toasted and/or roasted. However, taste should be considered. The roasting part should be affectionate, not critical or demeaning. For everyone's sake including your own, run your eulogy past a few others for their "take" on how appropriate it is. Funny, warm, and affectionate is one thing, biting is another. We've all been embarrassed at weddings when a best man flubs his speech. The same can happen in a eulogy, where it's even more inappropriate. Be smart, protect yourself, and be respectful to the bereaved. Honesty is fine, as long as it's good natured.

Interestingly, it used to be that there were few or no eulogies. And in fact, the Catholic Church does not permit them as part of a funeral, although friends and relatives can say a few words at a vigil or reception after the funeral. A funeral used to be considered a solemn event, led by a clergyman who probably had some relationship with the family. But as we've become a more secular society, that's not necessarily true anymore. Eulogies were unheard of when I was growing up. The family engaged a rabbi (usually one we didn't know—we were secular Jews who only attended services on the "high holidays"). The bereaved spoke to the rabbi (who probably never met the deceased) and provided the information needed for a sermon that indicated some knowledge of the person.

Be sure to include words about how much the deceased meant to you, as well. You could also talk about what you'll miss, now that he's gone (injecting some humor there, too). Then run the eulogy past a family member or friend to get feedback, if any. You can also practice in front of a mirror. Remember to ask yourself, "What's the worst that can happen?" If you blunder, you can just treat it with a sense of humor, too. People will appreciate it. They're probably also terrified of public speaking. Most of us are. So was Winston Churchill (who lisped), actor Bruce Willis (a stutterer), and even Warren Buffett when he was starting out.

For content of the eulogy, subjects to cover include (1) When and how you met. (2) The comfort of old friends (now lost). Maybe you were both on the same wavelength and could communicate with a look. You "got" each other. (3) Memories: Keep a pad handy and reminisce. Jot down the good times. (4) Look at photo albums and use the pictures to help you recall. Maybe you'll find a photo of your firstborn in the bathtub with your friend's child at age three. There's incredible nourishment and satisfaction in such reminders of happy days in the past.

Not all memories will be welcome. In one family, for example, factions fumed over whether to mention the deceased's overcoming an alcohol problem years earlier. Some bereaved saw it as evidence of the person's courage. Other family members were appalled and felt it sullied his image. In such cases a pastor or family friend may be able to help bridge differences.

There's a clash of cultures today between older and younger generations' attitudes toward online communication, religious rituals, and privacy. How much is too much honesty in a eulogy? Has a confrontation with the sorrow of death been eliminated by the "celebration" of the person's life? These are important questions to consider. The word *God* may never be mentioned in a service today, such as at a humanist funeral. A sense of mourning can be lost when a memorial service becomes too show biz or party-like.

17. What do you do if you're asked (or expected) to give a eulogy for a friend or family member, yet feel too overcome to speak? I'm okay writing a eulogy, but I don't want to face an audience.

Most of us fear public speaking in general, let alone when someone important to us has died. In fact, at most funerals I've attended, those closest to the deceased do not give eulogies. Many bereaved feel overcome enough by the loss without adding the pressure of a speech. One answer is to ask someone else to read the eulogy you've written. Your "stand in" can begin by explaining that you asked him or her to do so.

18. Is it okay to watch a live streaming or a webcast of a funeral instead of attending in person?

This is another "It depends" answer. Are you watching because it's more convenient for you? Or are you watching because it's impossible for you to be there due to illness (yours or a loved one's), travel issues (including costs, job commitments, or obligations), or interference with a vacation? If you're in Tahiti on the trip of a lifetime, it may not be possible to return in time for the services. Or perhaps you don't feel a strong enough connection to the deceased or bereaved to ruin your vacation.

If the deceased is a loved one, you might pay an emotional toll for the convenience of watching a funeral or memorial service on a laptop or cozied up on a couch at home. Rituals comfort us, connect us, enrich us—and watching them online (unless there's no other choice) can exact a big price, such as loss of community and the opportunity to share grief and humanity with others. It's one thing if it's the funeral of a public figure or someone peripheral in your life, but it's another thing if you're taking an easy way out. It's important to our emotional health to come together with others who loved or revered the deceased and share grief. Telling stories about the deceased and recalling good (and sometimes bad) times is healing. It reflects and reinforces our humanity.

In business situations, the price is lost personal contact with the bereaved. Your boss or colleague or client or customer may not notice your absence, but it's a sure thing that your presence would be observed and appreciated.

Streaming and webcasting technology does have a place in funeral services, and a video of the funeral service might be provided by funeral homes or places of worship, allowing family and friends to see it later. Videos can be quite innovative. In the case of a Florida motorcycle club member who died in his thirties, a drone videoed fellow bikers paying their respects, including a twenty-one-gun salute.

CONDOLENCES IN PERSONAL RELATIONSHIPS

19. What exactly are condolences, and why are they important?

Most of us have a general, though often vague, idea of what condolences actually are. Moreover, we ask too much of ourselves when we want to extend sympathy. Sometimes our own anxiety gets in the way. It helps to understand the definition of the word *condolence*, which derives from the Latin: "to feel another's pain, to grieve with." Condolences are expressions of sympathy or sorrow with the bereaved. They're a custom handed down through the ages to acknowledge a death and show support. We gather. We show up in words, gestures, and with our presence. Once upon a time, families and friends lived close by—down the road, up the block, or around the corner. Even if some moved elsewhere, they kept in close touch—and they gathered together at the time of a death (which usually occurred at home). Death was less mysterious in those days because it was a part of life. Family members and friends surrounded the bereaved and helped tend to the funeral and other details. They were also in a position to provide emotional support to the bereaved because they were part of the family's or neighborhood's everyday life. The support came naturally and was effective because there was knowledge of the family's needs.

Today, that kind of community is rare. Denial and discomfort with the idea of death is common—and death is likely to occur in a hospital or nursing home. We are no longer intimately acquainted with the death of our loved ones, and increasingly seem to distance ourselves from what used to be an intimate and natural experience. Condolence cards emerged in the nineteenth century to help folks maintain their social connections. The expression of concern to someone who is experiencing deep grief links us together and reinforces our sense of community. We can show that we are personally affected by another person's loss and suffering. We can openly empathize, show we care, and lend support. The message is that we know what has happened and we pay our respects as fellow human beings. This kind of communication is as important to us as it is to the bereaved.

Many people think they must say something eloquent and somehow banish the sadness of the bereaved. Yet the fact is you can't really provide comfort unless you have a very close relationship with the bereaved (or had one with the deceased). The rest of us merely need to connect, as in "I send my deepest condolences. You are in my thoughts." No one can make someone else's grief disappear or fix what has happened. Dead is dead. However, we can listen.

Perhaps the toughest condolences to extend orally or in writing are those to the bereaved you don't know well. They may be business or professional connections, or they may be acquaintances in your private life. Keep it simple. You know the person's loved one has died, but you don't know important details, such as the nature of the relationship, the depth of the bereaved's sadness, or the circumstances of death.

20. When is texting or email acceptable for condolences?

Well . . . it's complicated. Personally, I believe that texting can seem to trivialize what has happened. On the other hand, it's a fast, effective way to make contact and say, "I'm here." If the bereaved has notified you via email, texting, or social media, it's hard to fault you for following the lead. However, the gold standard is a handwritten condolence note. We all forget, too, that the bereaved (in a few weeks or a few months or even a year or two) will appreciate having tangible evidence of how thoughtful people were. The notes and cards can be revisited for years and even decades. They are timeless and attest to our humanity. Yet who saves online personal messages or even prints them out?

Another issue to consider: Is the bereaved comfortable with technology? I'd think twice before sending an email condolence to an elderly person who is not computer savvy.

That said, some obits today let you off the hook and invite you to visit a family's website or an online book of memories where you can share your thoughts about the deceased and/or express condolences to the bereaved.

Dos and Don'ts of Talking to the Bereaved

On the one hand:

- Don't ask what happened because the bereaved may feel forced to relive it.
- Don't mention a bereavement group right away. The bereaved may need a little time to get through the funeral first.
- Don't talk about when your (mother, brother, husband died). The bereaved isn't interested right now.
- Don't say, "I know someone who also lost a child." So what, and who cares?
- Don't ask, "Is there anything I can do?" It can enrage the bereaved because it shifts the "work" to the bereaved who is in shock and is in no condition to compile a to-do list for other people. It's also easy for the bereaved to feel you're "going through the motions" and that you really don't want to be bothered. In one case, when a new widow was asked that question, she suggested a favor that would be appreciated. The reply was: "Oh, I'd love to, but I'm going to _____ that day," or some other excuse. There are people you can rely on, and those you can't.
- Don't forget to consider what might be helpful to the bereaved as opposed to what's easiest for you. An example would be showing up at the front door of the bereaved's home with a pot of hot coffee and cookies from the bakery (or from your own oven). All you have to say is, "I thought you might like this." Don't stay unless the person seems to welcome your company. It's the gesture that counts. The person may really appreciate the coffee and cookies but might not feel like talking just then.
- Don't say anything religious unless you're a member of the same church or other place of worship. Do not assume the

person believes in God or heaven, and such. Do not mention God or heaven or religion unless you know the bereaved very well and are certain he or she will accept your observations. Remember, this is a secularized society and the ranks of the unaffiliated are growing steadily.

On the other hand:

- Do say, "He was an irreplaceable confidant and advisor." Or "She was my best friend. I'll miss her dearly."
- Use body language—a hug if you know the person well. If not, a touch on the arm.
- Mention who died, as in "I was sad to learn of your sister Sue's death."
- Send a note or gift basket to the bereaved you know. If you knew the deceased, but not the bereaved, send it to the closest relative.
- Use email to follow-up, as in "Just checking in to say 'Hello.'" Bereaved persons appreciate emails because they don't require the recipient to take any action. Yet they can help the bereaved feel connected and cared for.
- Do be careful of making assumptions. The widow or widower of an Alzheimer's patient may or may not feel relieved that the ordeal is over. The survivor may feel guilty about having been short tempered with the patient, rather than feeling relieved or set free. Also, realize the spouse has probably already done a lot of grieving.
- Say to the parent when a child has died, "My heart is with you." If you know the parent well, add, "I'm here for you." The worse the situation, the less there is to say.
- Do be short and simple. Try, "Please accept my condolences at this difficult time." If talking to the person on the phone, wait for his or her response. Let the bereaved take the lead.

21.

How do you find the right words to express condolences?

To feel more confident about expressing sympathy in person or in writing, simply recognize that the condolences are not about you. It's about putting yourself in another person's place and imagining how you would feel and what you would want to hear. Ask yourself these key questions:

Who is the bereaved?

And what is your relationship with the person? The more casual the connection, the briefer your words should be. You're going to write or converse differently, depending on whether the person is immediate family, extended family, a dear friend, a congenial neighbor, a boss, an employee, a colleague or coworker, your accountant, a customer or client—or an acquaintance at the PTA or the gym.

Who died?

Today sixty is much younger than it used to be. Many people live for two or three more decades—and some even longer. You'll write or say something different if the deceased died at ninety-eight. That's a long life. Nobody lives forever. Yet the grief of the bereaved is personal and loss is loss.

Who can imagine losing a child, or even an adult child to a sudden fatal illness or injury? Regardless of your age, it's unnatural to survive your child—think of the photos of the

106-year-old mother of Arizona senator John McCain at his memorial services.

How did the deceased die?

Sudden deaths grab us by the throat and fill us with despair and disbelief because they happen from out of the blue, without warning. The deceased may have been as healthy as a horse, strong and robust, and sometimes young. There is no time for the bereaved to prepare for the shock, to ease into the idea that the person is gone. A recent college graduate, thrilled after landing her dream job, doesn't return home from work—the victim of a highway collision. A nine-year-old hangs himself in his bedroom after bouts of relentless   bullying by schoolmates. A forty-five-year-old skier suffers a massive heart attack on the slopes. My own next door neighbor choked to death at dinner one night. "This is unbelievable!" comes to mind as an appropriate condolence response.

But the right words for one person can inflame someone else. Below, I've tried to present strategies that will work most the time.

In person—what to say at the funeral or a related event such as a visitation

My rule is to say as little as possible. If you know the bereaved well, a hug can say it all. Then wait for the bereaved to speak and follow the person's lead. This is the time to use your listening skills. Usually, the worst mistakes are made by people who feel afraid, mortified, or uncomfortable about greeting the bereaved in person, whether at the funeral or another service—or on the street. We tend to talk too much because we feel anxious and want to fill the silence. This can lead to blurting something inappropriate, such as, "You're lucky to have had her for sixteen years." The bereaved is unlikely to feel that way. These are the last statements the bereaved wants to hear. Instead, a quiet touch on the arm is worth a hundred words. Or simply say, "My condolences." Or "Please accept my condolences." Then hold your tongue and give the bereaved a chance to respond. Expect a moment of silence first, which is hard for many of us to tolerate. That's why it's a good idea to rehearse first at home to build your confidence.

What to say in writing

The safest and easiest approach is to stick to the basics and keep your message short unless you are or were very close to the bereaved/deceased. Two or three lines can be enough, as in "Dear _____, Ed told me about your (mother's, brother's, spouse's) death. Know that I am thinking of you at this difficult time. With deepest sympathy." (Add your signature.) Or "I just heard of (loved one's) death. Please accept my sincere condolences," and add your signature.

If you try to write anything longer, you boost the risk of offending. Another option is, "Dear _____, Please accept my deepest condolences on the death of _____ . My thoughts are with you and your family." (Follow with your signature.)

22. How can I avoid condolence disasters?

In his book *Getting Grief Right: Finding Your Story of Love in the Sorrow of Loss*, grief counselor and educator Patrick O'Malley, PhD, notes that some people possess "grief literacy." However, the majority of us lack such skills.

Basically, say as little as possible and assume nothing about how the bereaved must be feeling. Do not offer advice, especially at the funeral, unless asked for it. You're not in a position to give it unless you are extremely close to the bereaved. No matter how the bereaved complained about her mother or father or sibling, that doesn't mean the person isn't crushed by the death. Some people actually forget all their complaints about the deceased after the death. I've seen it happen multiple times. So don't make jokes in the vein of, "Well now you won't have listen to all her demands anymore." The bereaved may feel bereft or guilty or who knows what, regardless of how much they complained while the person was alive.

Here's an example of a condolence disaster. One woman told me, "When the husband of a friend of a friend suddenly died recently, I felt shocked and asked for the bereaved's address in order to send a condolence card. I wrote that, although I did not know them well, I could see they were devoted to each other. Subsequently I learned that he had blown his head off. She had tried to stop him, and he did it right in front of her. I feel like a jerk for sending that card. I wish I could take it back."

If you don't know the bereaved or the deceased well, do not write more than a line or two. If the writer had just said, after expressing shock, "We send our deepest sympathy" and signed the note, it would have been appropriate. "I can't imagine what you're going through" works, too. It's always dangerous to comment on a couple's relationship with each other as an acquaintance—you know little or nothing about their private life.

Most condolence disasters are about the writer's anxiety—not the bereaved. If your connection to the deceased or the bereaved is distant, then it stands to reason the bereaved won't expect to hear from you. If you meet on the street, of course you would have to say something. But it isn't necessary to send a card in such cases. These can be treacherous waters.

23. I've heard that some people take offense at the words, "I'm sorry for your loss." Why is that? And what is a "safer" thing to say? I want to commiserate, not anger the bereaved.

"I'm sorry for your loss" is a common and accepted way to express condolences. The words "I'm sorry" convey compassion, empathy (sharing the experience in some way), and solace. In these changing times, however, everything is fair game for accusation. Some expressions might be considered cliché or otherwise trite and annoying. Particularly with the advent of social media, it's become anathema for some younger people to hear (or say to others), "I'm sorry." Their view is, "What are you sorry about? Why are you apologizing? My mother had a fatal heart attack. It had nothing to do with you. You're not to blame." The bereaved's patience is stretched thin or gone entirely. On the other hand, the same people may be quite comfortable hearing, "This sucks."

Some also contend that "I'm sorry" isolates the bereaved, and is equivalent to saying you just lost your reading glasses or "Have a nice day." Other issues are the facts of what happened. "I'm sorry for your loss" can seem truly inadequate if the death is sudden or a tragedy. It's always been a challenge to extend sympathy to the bereaved at a funeral or memorial service—or write words of condolence on a card. But it's trickier than ever now, and the right words can vary depending on the age group. Acceptable things to say (and the medium in which to say them) may now be considered inappropriate by some people. Statements that once seemed inconceivable may now be okay.

I've become more sensitive to these distinctions, and unless I know the bereaved very well, I say something like, "Please accept my condolences (or deep sympathy)." In the case of a school shooting or other massacre, you can just say it like it is:

"This is a catastrophe" or "There are no words." Or "How could this happen?" Such words are also appropriate in the case of unexpected death—say a hit and run. They mirror what the bereaved is probably feeling. If the death is more routine—say, an elderly parent or an aunt or uncle died, I might say something like, "This is a sad day."

24. What's the best way to respond when the death is a tragedy or suicide?

Tragedies come in all forms, but some are particularly hard to fathom. What do you say if a six-year-old has died in a freak accident? In the documentary *Pope Francis: A Man of His Word*, Pope Francis describes his strategy for communicating with world leaders as being: "Talk little. Listen a lot." I think this approach also applies for responding to devastating loss. One bereaved parent told me, "Don't say anything. Just hold my hand."

Suicide in Our Society

Suicide does not discriminate. It shows up on Park Avenue, affecting those who "have everything." It happens in Middle America. It takes public figures and private citizens, the rich and the poor. It is the tenth leading cause of death in the United States. Most of those who die by suicide do not have a diagnosed mental problem.

Between 1999 and 2016 (the latest year for which figures are available), the suicide rate in the United States jumped 25 percent, according to the Centers for Disease Control and Prevention (CDC). Almost 45,000 Americans aged ten and older killed themselves in 2016. Women's suicide rates jumped almost 60 percent in the forty-five to sixty-four age group (a low point for life satisfaction and time of increased stress and depression) from 2000 to 2016, according to the CDC.

What do you write to the bereaved in a suicide death? Realize that what's different is the deceased deliberately made the choice to die. Bereaved parents and other loved ones commonly feel anger, denial, and shock. They agonize, "Could I have prevented it?"

On the other hand, some bereaved may even feel relieved in cases where the deceased suffered with mental problems for years, and they may take comfort in knowing that the struggle is at an end. Every case is different. Acknowledge the devastating loss with: "This is inconceivable" or "There are no words for this heartbreak." And then shut up.

Understand the helplessness of all concerned. Parents feel they've failed to protect their precious child. It's impossible to "fix it" or change reality or diminish grief. It is what it is.

Do not ask questions. Instead, allow the bereaved to lead you. Later, if you know the person well, it's okay to say, "Do you feel like talking?" Then just stay quiet or add, "I'm a good listener." Hopefully, parents will experience diminishing despair as they live through the process of accepting the loss and find emotional balance. At some point you can eventually say something like, "There's a nonprofit organization called Compassionate Friends that supports parents, siblings, and grandparents after the death of a child. There are 600 chapters in the United States, plus chapters in thirty countries. Here's the website address if you want to take a look." Then say no more. For reference, the web address is compassionatefriends.org.

25. What do I say when someone loses an elderly parent?

The death of elderly parents is an expected loss in our society. This prospect tends to soften the effect of grief on bereaved adult children. For example, the adult "child" might be told by a spouse or others to just "Get over it." However, research shows that the surviving adult children can have a very hard time with the loss. A mother's death can have a more negative effect on daughters than sons. The death of an older father is harder on an adult son. In either case, the bereaved has lost not only a key person in the parent but a central life role as a son or a daughter.

A great way to go with condolences is to reflect, if possible, on how much the parent loved and was proud of the adult child, as in, "Your mom always said you were a fabulous son. She could count on you. You'd never let her down." Another parent quote might be, "Your father was your biggest fan. He was always bragging about you."

Another approach is to talk about your own experience of the parent, as in, "I always admired your mom. She adored you." Or "I always smile when I think of your mom. I still use her recipe for brownies."

26. What should I say to someone whose beloved cat just died? I'm not a pet person and it feels kind of weird to offer condolences.

People who are not, and who never have been, pet owners can wonder at the human trauma to owners when a pet dies—and fail to appreciate the depth of the owner's loss.

According to the American Pet Products Association's 2017–18 survey of pet owners, more than half of dog and cat owners view their pets as family members. Owners buy pet health insurance for almost 9,000,000 dogs and 4,700,000 cats. Veterinary costs, like health care expenditures for humans, are up, too—10 percent for treatments and 5 percent for checkups.

Owners spent a total of $69.5 billion on pets in 2017. And, like us, the older they get the greater their need for medical care.

Attachments to animal companions can be as strong as relationships with people. According to the Hospice Foundation of America, pet owners can experience extreme grief and sadness. I personally know a survivor of 9/11 who, despite antidepressants, therapy, and other remedies, could barely function—until she bought a dog. He was literally a lifesaver. When he died unexpectedly, the loss was monumental to her.

In such a case, I would say something like, "I know that (name of animal) meant so much to you. He helped you live a life again." Then allow the owner to speak. This is also a time when an email condolence note does the job. If you were a neighbor of the owner and saw the pet regularly, you can also reminisce, as in, "She was always so cute, even her bark was adorable—and so devoted to you."

27. What's a condolence "gift"?

Flowers, a plant, a food platter, or fruit basket all qualify. Some people even send a book that relates to grief and mourning that the bereaved can pick up and read at some point in the future. However, be careful not to choose a title with religious overtones unless you know the bereaved very well and are certain the text is appropriate for the situation.

In some communities it's a tradition to enclose money or a check with a condolence card to help pay funeral expenses. Today, however, crowdfunding can provide another way to aid a family in need. (See Question 76: "How can I crowdfund a funeral or memorial service—and why is it so popular these days?" on page 107.) If you want to write a note or send flowers or give another item to the bereaved but don't know the address, check the obituary to see if it includes this information. If not, call the funeral home. They should be able to help you.

28. What should I know about contacting the bereaved after the funeral and other events are over?

After the urgency and attention of the first few weeks, people tend to forget about the survivors left behind. Yet this is the very time the bereaved can begin to feel very alone and/or isolated and need support. Six months later, it can feel to them as if everyone is gone. If you can't make the funeral, visit or call a month or two later to show you care. Perhaps suggest coffee or lunch if you wish. As a tragic example, a woman's fiancé died of a blood clot a few days before their wedding. He was thirty. Some of her friends went on vacation with her on the sixth month anniversary of his death.

29. What can I say in a sympathy note to the family of an industry colleague?

Career-related condolences can be difficult because there may or may not be a personal connection involved. How about something like, "We knew of Bill's illness, which may have prepared us somewhat. But his loss is real and can only be soothed by many wonderful memories of working together. Deepest sympathies from your many friends at (name of company)."

Or "Dear (name of widow), I think we last met on a plane to London where we separated to depart for different vacation destinations. I knew Joe for over twenty years and valued him both as a colleague and friend. I cannot imagine the practice without his humor, laughter, and ability to share family war stories. I will miss him. To you and yours my deepest condolences."

Or "We read of Mary's death and were sorry we were unable to attend services. I remember her well. We did business together for many years. We're happy we were able to spend good times with both of you. Please extend our deepest condolences to the entire family. Sincerely," and add your signature. Or "Our thoughts and prayers are with you and the entire family."

Or "Jim is a man for whom I had the greatest admiration

and affection. He was a true friend." Or "Bob will be missed by so many here. He was a gentleman." Or "Our company seems to have always been dealing from a position of strength because Sheila was there and involved. In addition to her energy and knowledge, she also brought great balance and a sense of humor."

Any and all of these sentiments can be handwritten at the bottom of a condolence greeting card or as a note on a correspondence card.

Cheat Sheet: What to Write to the Family of a Deceased Colleague

- The world lost a great doctor and we lost a dear friend when Charley died. You are in my/our thoughts and prayers.
- Over the months he was ill, I heard one statement repeatedly: Patrick will be a hard act to follow. Please know that I'm thinking of you in your sorrow.
- Helen was an important mentor to me and always kind. I'll miss her good advice.
- Janet always entertained me with her stories, her laugh, and her smile—and she was a consummate sales professional, a trusted friend. I'll truly miss her. Much love to you at this saddest of times.
- We will always remember the good days. We were away when Lee died. We wish you and your daughter strength during this difficult time. We send our condolences.
- What a loss! Jerry was unique. We'll treasure the memories of our adventures together, both professional and personal. We send you our love.

- I'm so sorry to learn of the death of your mother. Please accept my sincere condolences. Take care. Sincerely, _____.
- I just read the Society's message board about your brother's death. Please know that you have my deepest sympathy.
- Gil was a superb teacher. His students adored him and his colleagues respected him. He will be sorely missed by us all. Please extend my sympathy to your entire family.
- Working with Marian has meant a lot to me. She was demanding of her young associates, yet generous at the same time. My recent promotion wouldn't have been possible without her help and guidance.

30.

What if I've never met a bereaved customer in person, although we've done business on the phone and via email for years? Can I send a printed condolence card?

Absolutely. But personalize it by adding a handwritten line or two, such as "You're in my thoughts at this sad time." If you want to cement the relationship, why not make a donation in memory of the deceased to charity. The bereaved will be notified of your contribution with a card reading, "The (name of charity) informs you that (name of company or just your name) has made a contribution in memory of (name of deceased)." The amount donated is not disclosed, and you can send whatever you feel comfortable with.

On the other hand, beware of cases where the deceased was

(or the bereaved is) a prospective customer or client you barely know. Lack of condolences from you will not be noticed. However, their presence can make the bereaved feel you are trying to ingratiate yourself and "woo" business for the future. In one case, a real estate broker, who had showed the bereaved an apartment, sent a condolence card with a business card enclosed. The recipient, whose spouse had died, felt the broker hoped she'd sell her present apartment and purchase a smaller place. A condolence card is not an opportunity to conduct business.

Incidentally, lists of right and wrong things to say abound on the Internet. In some cases one line is perfect for the bereaved. However, the same words might upset someone else. In the end, I just do my best—and so should you.

31. How should I handle condolences to a client from a whole department or group at my company?

"On behalf of the employees at XYZ Corporation, we send our condolences to you and your family. Ginny was a rare individual who was always there for us when we had a question or problem. (Mention the work connection and describe her attributes.) She will be missed by those of us at (name of company) who had the pleasure to know her. The company has made a donation in her memory to (name of charity)." The message was followed by the signatures of five people.

"The Board of Directors of _____ extend to you and your family our heartfelt sympathy. Bill touched all of our lives in a most profound way. We will all miss his guidance, wit, but most of all his wonderful smile. Our sincere condolences, XYZ Association, John Smith President."

"Joe will be sorely missed by all of us at ABC Company. I extend my personal condolences to you and your family."

"We just learned the sad news of your loss. We not only considered Frank a colleague, but also a friend. Heartfelt condolences to you and your family."

One company sent a large card with short messages, such as "He was an inspiration" and "I will miss his 'smarts' and friendship," handwritten by fourteen different people.

32. What are the rules for business-related In Memoriams?

In some cases, in addition to the family's obituary, multiple "In Memoriams" are placed by employers, employees, family friends, or organizations that have benefited from the deceased's financial support or contribution of time and effort (as in the case of a board member of a charity or cause). The wording may be something like, "The staff and Board of Directors mourn the passing (or the death) of _____" Or "Our condolences go out to the family of _____" Or "We are deeply saddened by the passing of our dear friend and supporter _____." Or "Her many contributions will live on in our memories."

33. What should a company say when placing newspaper In Memoriam display ads for a client, business connections, or the firm's leader or board member?"
Two publishers ran In Memoriam display ads when a prestigious author died. Each company had published his works. Both ads featured the author's name, followed by the years of birth and death. One ad included a quote from one of his books. The other ad simply stated, "A Great American Writer" underneath.

Another In Memoriam display ad featured a quote by Daniel Webster, followed by "In Memory of Our Beloved Partner (name of deceased)." Yet another In Memoriam ad read, "(Name of company) celebrates the legacy of (name of affiliate and friend of the firm, followed by dates of birth and death)." The name and logo of the organization appeared as the signature below.

In Memoriam display ads, which are often "bordered" by a black line framing the edge, may also say something like,

"Smith & Co. celebrates the legacy of (name of deceased),"
followed by the birth and death dates. Or "In memory of our
founding partner." The organization logo then follows. The ad
may or may not include a photograph of the deceased. Another
option is to use a meaningful quote from a famous philoso-
pher, author, or statesman at the top of the ad. I like this quote
from Emily Dickinson: "Because I could not stop for Death—
/ He kindly stopped for me— / The Carriage held but just
Ourselves— / And Immortality."

34. I plan to attend a coworker's funeral, but
should I go to the viewing or visitation, too?
I didn't know him well (or his family at all), but we
exchanged pleasantries over the years.

The viewing or visitation is usually held a day before the
funeral. The body of the deceased may be present. It's up to
you to decide which of these events, if any, you want to attend.
One way to handle it is to check with colleagues and see what
they are doing.

In addition, don't make a snap decision until you read the
obituary or call the funeral home for information. It may turn
out you're off the hook if the viewing is private and restricted to
family members only. If you need to choose between a visitation
or the funeral, remember the latter is the most important event.

"STICKY" CONDOLENCES

35. Should I attend my ex-spouse's funeral? I never trashed him to my kids, and I'd like to be there to support them at a sad time in their lives. What's the right thing to do?

Although some etiquette experts advise skipping it as a rule of thumb, my position is, "It depends." If you want to support your children who have just lost their father, by all means do so. But stay in the background. If you had an amicable divorce, why not? If your ex had children from a previous marriage with whom you maintained a cordial relationship, why not?

However, if there are issues (such as you don't speak to the current spouse), why go? In short, a funeral doesn't need any extra human complications. If there's going to be discomfort for anyone, why not simply make a donation in memory of the deceased and have the charity acknowledge the contribution to the people you specify?

That said, I know several people who attended their ex's memorial service or funeral. If you're determined to go, then go with the right attitude and be considerate. Remember that no matter how messy the divorce, your children have just lost a parent. Unfortunately, not everyone behaves like an adult. I know of one former wife who greeted her ex's widow at the funeral home with the words, "Now you know what it's like to lose your husband." The widow did have an affair with the deceased while he was married to the ex, which led to the divorce. However . . .

36. A neighbor and I stopped talking years ago after an altercation over property boundaries. I just heard her husband was killed in an accident and I'm torn. I want to send her a condolence note or even flowers, but I don't know what to say. We had a bitter split and it's been a long time. Do you have any suggestions?

I think you must ask yourself a few questions, beginning with, "Why do I want to contact her now?" Has the death made you feel guilty that you overreacted years ago? Does the original matter seem trivial now, given perspective? It may now seem silly in the face of death. Are you wondering, "Why did I make such a big deal about it?" Another question to consider is: "Was the surviving spouse involved in the dispute?" If not and your beef was with the deceased, then there's no reason not to send condolences. However, if the spouse was involved, you might want to think twice about extending sympathy. Ultimately, you must decide if you are trying to soothe your own conscience about overreacting long ago, or if you are trying to offer support to the spouse. Once you've made that determination in light of these other considerations, proceed accordingly.

37.

A former neighbor just died, and I really liked him. I want to make a donation in his memory, but I am not a fan of the charity suggested in the obituary. Can I contribute to something I consider worthier? Also, how much should I donate? I don't want to be embarrassed by sending too small an amount.

Remember, this is not about you. It's about the deceased and the bereaved. If at all possible, their wishes should be respected. One option might be to donate to a charity connected with the cause of death, such as the American Heart Association, if someone died of heart failure, or the cancer center where the deceased was treated. The deceased's alma mater is another idea. The point is, the donation should make some sense. You may be a cat lover, but that doesn't mean giving to the ASPCA is appropriate in this instance.

That said, I recently saw one obit that solved the problem. The wording was, "Donations should be made to the charity of your choice." If you can't find something that works for both you and the bereaved, consider giving a fruit basket.

Be aware, too, that the charity or institution or cause will send an acknowledgment of your gift to the bereaved without mentioning the amount donated. Whatever the size, you needn't worry about giving too little. Note, too, that donations to an IRS-accepted charity or cause are tax deductible.

38. I want to commemorate a dear friend who recently died, but I'd like to do something different than contributing to the usual charities or institutions. Any suggestions?

A few. How about the USDA Forest Service Plant-a-Tree Program? You can donate as little as $10 to plant about ten seedlings. No specific tree memorializes a particular individual. The funds are pooled for use where they are most urgently needed, and your gift is tax deductible. In view of all the devastating forest fires in recent years, planting trees is a wonderful gesture in memory of someone important to you.

Another choice is The Trees Remember, which works through nonprofit conservation groups to plant trees on US National Forest lands and on public lands destroyed by forest fires. Here you can dedicate a particular tree and may be able to pick the forest. Trees can be planted in Israel, as well, for as little as $18. There is even a Coretta Scott King Forest in northern Israel where tree donations can be made.

Other possibilities abound. At colleges today, you can often donate memorial plaques that will be put on seats in sports stadiums. For example, at the United States Naval Academy, you can name a seat (or as many as ten seats) at the Navy-Marine Corps Memorial Stadium for $1,000 each in its Take-A-Seat program. The plaque, which can be in memory of alumni, family, or friends, can carry up to four lines of twenty-six characters each. No alumni status is required, and there are no real limitations for where the seats are located. Plaques can also be placed on up to five seats in the Max Bishop Baseball Stadium and at Alumni Hall. The memorials continue in perpetuity—no need to renew payment.

A friend of mine "bought" a bench in Central Park, where a plaque commemorates her late husband. In San Mateo County, California, you can commemorate a bench or picnic table for a donation of $5,000 or more for a loved one for ten years—or $8,500 for twenty years. The 3-by-12-inch plaque with several lines of text is inlaid into the bench or table board.

39. I'm attending a graveside service and celebration of life several months after the person died. I made a donation in memory of the deceased right after the death. Should I send flowers now?

It is not necessary, but it's up to you. However, a handwritten note is a nice idea. You might say something like, "I still can't believe George is gone. I miss him so much." Wording matters. Saying, "I miss him, too," could anger the bereaved, because it might be taken to mean you're comparing your grief to the bereaved's.

40. Is a donation in a business situation a good idea?

Yes. The bereaved will be notified of it. They will receive a card that says something like: "A gift has been recieved by (name of charity) in memory of (name of deceased). This thoughtful gesture was made by (name of organization, company, firm). We are grateful for this kind and caring tribute." No mention will be made of the amount.

FUNERAL GUIDE BY RELIGION

Public funeral rites comfort mourners and strengthen hope within us. Since ancient times, humans have observed a period of mourning between death and the disposition of the body. These rites help us cope with the unfathomable—the reality of death, loss, and our own deepest fears. They help us process what has happened, and say goodbye.

However, funerals can be tough even when you're familiar with the religion—let alone when you have little or no idea of what to expect. Someone else's place of worship can seem mysterious and maybe even scary. Each faith has its own attitudes toward funeral rites and how to view and process death. Today, in our multicultural society, the chances are greater than ever that you will attend services in a religion other than your own, including some that can seem truly unusual. The good news is congregations tend to go out of their way to welcome a diversity of attendees at funeral and memorial services. Note, too, that there may be variations in services in individual congregations of the same religion. Attend with the attitude of respect for the bereaved and deceased, and strive to honor that religion in the individual person.

According to the Religious Landscape Study by the Pew Research Center, 70.6 percent of Americans are Christian. This includes Evangelical Protestant (25.4 percent); mainline Protestant (14.7 percent); historically black Protestant (6.5 percent); Catholic (20.8 percent); Mormon (1.6 percent);

Orthodox Christian (0.5 percent); Jehovah's Witness (0.8 percent); and other Christian (0.4 percent). The breakdown in other faiths is Jewish (1.9 percent); Muslim (0.9 percent); Buddhist (0.7 percent); Hindu (0.7 percent); other world Religions (0.3 percent); and unaffiliated (22.8 percent). The rest are atheist, agnostic, nothing in particular, or don't know.

Buddhist

41. **What should I know about a Buddhist funeral?**
Buddha (the name means "one who is enlightened") was a monk, sage, and teacher who lived 2,600 years ago. Buddhists believe that death of the body is not the end. Instead, the spirit continues and is reborn (reincarnation). The family will be at the funeral home or temple before the funeral. Expect chants and prayers, which are intended to help the deceased make the journey ahead. In some temples you may sit on the floor on meditation cushions.

If there's a wake, the body may or may not be embalmed. (Some Buddhists wish to be cremated.) The casket is open at the wake, and you are expected to view it. There are major differences in customs, depending on the country of origin and the sect.

Services, which can be scheduled before or after burial or cremation, may be held at home or at a funeral home. Either monks or families officiate. Both men and women dress casually in loose clothing. No head covering is necessary. The bereaved usually wear white or dark colors, depending on the tradition followed.

If you wish to make a donation, you will be asked to help defray funeral expenses. You can ring bells, and you can bring fruit and/or flowers.

Catholic

42. What should a non-Catholic know before attending a Catholic funeral?

Catholic funeral rites focus on faith, hope, belief in eternal life, that the soul lives on, and the resurrection of the body. The funeral usually takes place within a few days of the death, although it may be up to a week later. A vigil service or wake is typically held during the visitation or viewing at a funeral home, church, the family's home, or other venue. The cremains or the body is present. The body lies in an open or closed casket. This is an opportunity to pay your respects and offer your condolences to the bereaved.

Mass is the central act of worship of the Roman Catholic church. At a funeral mass, the body or cremains are present, and the special prayers of a mass are included. In contrast, the body or cremated remains are not present at a memorial mass. Funeral masses are not permitted in funeral homes, although the funeral liturgy outside of mass is allowed. A funeral mass usually lasts an hour or so. A memorial mass is about half as long. Incense is used at a Catholic funeral as a sign of respect and as a symbol of prayers rising to heaven.

How should you behave at the funeral? If you are not Catholic, do not take communion. You can sit wherever you wish. Stand when others do. However, you needn't genuflect (kneel at least one knee to the ground), cross yourself, or read prayers if you feel uncomfortable about it. If there is an open casket, you are expected to view the body. However, you can just quietly pass by, following others.

Standards of dress have relaxed these days, but to be sure you'll fit in, dress in dark, conservative, clothing. A jacket and tie for men is always right.

The final ceremony is the rite of committal, which concludes the funeral. It usually occurs at the cemetery, at the open grave, or at the place of interment.

43. What is a mass card?

Anyone (Catholic or not) can send a mass card to a Catholic bereaved as a gesture of respect. You can buy the card (which is essentially a donation to the church) at the church or even online. The card promises that prayers (or a mass for the deceased's soul) will be said on a date to be arranged with the bereaved.

44. I thought a Catholic couldn't be cremated, but I've heard that's no longer true? How come?

Times have changed. The Catholic Church eliminated its ban on cremation in 1963, although its preference for burial remained. In 1997, the church also began to allow a funeral after cremation (rather than only beforehand) to permit the bereaved to fully mourn. However, ashes cannot be scattered or placed in an urn on the mantle at home or made into jewelry.

Cremains must be buried or entombed in a mausoleum or placed in a columbarium niche, preferably in a Catholic cemetery.

45. Is it true that eulogies cannot be said at a Catholic funeral?

Yes. However, eulogies are encouraged at the vigil, which follows the death, but occurs before the funeral mass and burial. Friends and family may also speak at the reception or luncheon (if any) following the funeral.

46. Must I attend more than just the funeral?

A close friend might. Others will probably attend the funeral only. If you do attend a visitation or viewing held before the funeral, be punctual and don't linger. The family must deal with the funeral details for the next day.

Hindu

47. I'm going to a Hindu funeral service. How can I avoid doing or saying anything dis-respectful? Hindus believe in reincarnation and that the soul is reborn in various forms after death. Eventually it finds its true form, which can be an animal, insect, or even a plant.

Hindus are cremated, which is believed to purify the body, within the next dusk or dawn after the death, whichever is sooner. The body is placed in a coffin and then proceeds to the cremation.

In the United States, the cremation must take place in a crematorium. The cremains are often scattered in a lake, river, or other body of water.

Women need not cover their heads, but modesty is essential. For example, sleeveless apparel and miniskirts are taboo. A white shirt is fine for men. The family can't cook for a day or more after cremation, so others prepare food.

A period of mourning follows cremation and ends on the morning of the thirteenth day afterward.

48.

What should I expect at a Jewish funeral—
and what is "shiva"?

Separate Jewish ethnic communities share a tradition yet have their own practices. According to the Berkley Center for Religion, Peace & World Affairs, over 75 percent of Jews are Ashkenazi (German-descended), and 20 percent are Sephardim, who originate in the Iberian Peninsula and Arabic lands. In the United States, the largest denomination of Jews (about 38 percent) are Reformed Jews, who seek to combine innovation and tradition; 33 percent are Conservative; and 22 percent Orthodox. Customs are in flux, as in other religions today.

Jewish funerals are usually held within twenty-four to forty-eight hours of death. Cremation is becoming more accepted. There is no visitation before the funeral, although the bereaved are usually available for up to an hour before the funeral service at the funeral home. The funeral can last anywhere from fifteen to sixty minutes. Dress in dark colors and conservatively—a jacket and tie for men is appropriate, though individual temples may be more casual. Women wear skirts, pants, dresses, with sleeves of any length, but necklines should be modest.

Reformed Jews may not wear a yarmulke or kippah (a skullcap) in synagogue. In Orthodox and Conservative congregations, women's heads may be covered. Yarmulkes are usually available as you enter a synagogue or funeral home. However, there is no mandate to wear one. Crosses or other religious jewelry should not be worn. Services are held at a funeral home or synagogue and the casket is always closed. A rabbi officiates and a cantor sings. In the past the rabbi usually gave the eulogy, although that is changing. Family members and friends now often give eulogies for the deceased.

If you are not Jewish, all you have to do is stand when the congregation does so. Do not send flowers to the funeral location or to the home of the bereaved.

Shiva is the mourning tradition of Jewish people, and it begins immediately after the funeral. The custom is called "sitting shiva." Shiva usually takes place for seven days in the home of the bereaved, although some have shortened it recently. It is a custom that helps the bereaved process the death by allowing them to mourn and remember together, and then return to normal life. This tradition asks the bereaved to stop what they normally do, sit together, think about the person who died, and experience each other. However, someone who is sick is not required to follow the rules.

Expect to wash your hands either as you leave the cemetery (if you go to the graveside) and/or before entering the shiva home. The door is usually left open for visitors, who simply walk in. Mourners should not be addressed until they talk to you. (In the meantime you can talk quietly with other visitors.) A rabbi advises, "Never be the first to speak when greeting a newly bereaved. Just touch an arm or shoulder and wait for the person to say something. That will set the tone, and you'll be less likely to make a mistake." Visiting hours are sometimes mentioned in obituaries. If that is not the case, check with the funeral home or with a family member or close friend of the bereaved, or plan on visiting in the afternoon or early evening. Shiva is not observed on Shabbat, the day of rest, which begins at sundown Friday.

Plan on no more than a thirty-minute visit, unless you are family or a very close friend. This is no time to show up late at night. In one case, a grieving widow heard her doorbell ring at 10 p.m., long after visitors had left. She was exhausted and wore her nightgown and robe. Who were the callers? Casual acquaintances. And she was not glad to see them.

Although flowers are not appropriate, you can send baskets of fruit, candy, and baked goods like rugalach. Platters of traditional foods like delicatessen or appetizers (smoked fish, lox, and the like) are also appropriate. If you don't know whether the bereaved are kosher, find out. Or you can just play it safe and send kosher food—or stick to a fruit basket.

Muslim

49. What should I expect at a Muslim funeral?

Services are held at a funeral home or mosque, usually two days after death. Men sit in the front, women in the back. Expect the service to last thirty to sixty minutes. Men can wear a sports shirt and slacks. Women should dress modestly and choose dark colors. A scarf should cover the head. Jewelry such as a cross or Star of David should be left at home. Flowers or food can be sent to the home of the bereaved after the funeral or a donation can be made to a charity in memory of the deceased.

Cremation is forbidden and viewed as disrespectful. Do not expect a visitation or wake before the funeral because the body must be buried within two days or so. The body is not embalmed, and the casket is closed. An Imam leads the funeral prayers. There is no eulogy. Simplicity is a hallmark of Muslim funerals—and of the caskets used. Burial in the United States is often in an Islamic section of a cemetery. In some cases, where the deceased was born abroad, the costs of sending a body back to the deceased's country of birth for burial will be financed by that Muslim nation.

The bereaved can be visited at home. Phone calls are also permitted. The bereaved mourn for three days.

Protestant

50. What should I expect at a Protestant funeral?
With about 15,000,000 members, Southern Baptists are the largest Protestant denomination in the United

States. On one level Protestant beliefs and rituals aren't all that different from those of Catholicism, but each Protestant denomination varies a little bit in its rituals and rules.

Protestants believe in eternal life. Some churches do communion and some don't. However, there is a wake or visitation where people come to pay respects. Viewings are usually held on the afternoon or evening before the funeral. Friends and relatives can give eulogies at the funeral. However, funerals in some sects are not open to the public. Cremations are common. So are memorial services that take place a month or more after the death, because so many families are spread out.

As for the dress code, people do tend to dress in dark colors.

Humanist

51. What's a "humanist" funeral?

The humanism movement, which began during the Renaissance, is a system of values and beliefs based on the idea that people are basically good and we can solve problems using reason instead of religion. Humanists do not attend places of worship or want their funerals held there. However, a humanist (or nonreligious) service can be held in a funeral home—as well as outdoors or in any other setting of choice. The bereaved can pick and choose the order of service and which, if any, traditions they wish to follow. A wake may or may not be included. A funeral celebrant (see Question 66: "What's a 'funeral celebrant'?" on page 96) can help plan and run the service. Note that humanist funerals may or may not be "green." (See Question 62: "What exactly is a 'green funeral' and a 'green burial'—and why choose one?" on page 92.)

When You Are the Bereaved

Virtually all of us have attended funerals, but organizing one is another story, especially these days. Whole new ways of handling funerals, burials, cremations, and even mourning have emerged as a sign of the times. You can find yourself drowning in decisions large and small at the very same time you're grieving. The following information is here to help you cut through the confusion.

There are so many options today. Do you want to use a funeral home, run a home funeral, or do a green burial? Do you want to cremate and bury the ashes (or not) or scatter ashes—and if so, where? Or how about a memorial service (or two or three) at different times?

52. Why do memorial services seem to be so common these days?

Because so many deceased are cremated, there's no big rush to bury the body. The cremation rate in the United States is up to 50.2 percent and is expected to hit 79.1 percent by 2035, according to the National Funeral Directors Association (NFDA). In addition, cremations cost less than one-third the price of funerals with burials. The family can take time to plan and control the event, even waiting for better weather if the death occurs in winter up north or summer down south. The service can also be personalized to reflect who the person was. A memorial service can save money, too, because you can eliminate the cost of the hearse and many other funeral home charges. You can also choose a venue like a restaurant, hotel, or your home, if you're up to it.

It's not uncommon for some bereaved to schedule more than one memorial service at different times and places to accommodate friends and family members across the country. The issues involved include the venue, atmosphere, plus who and how many will attend or speak. We're all individuals and we all have different views of the deceased and ourselves. However, waiting a year to plan a celebration of life might invite criticism that the memory of the deceased is not being honored.

53. Can a funeral or memorial service be joyous?

Yes. Laughter, joy, music, and song may seem at odds with a funeral or memorial service. Yet "Celebrations of Life" are a new trend in mourning the dead. African and other cultures have always combined them, however—and jazz funerals in New Orleans are still big attractions.

A Ghanaian funeral today is a community party event. The service may not start until 10 p.m.—and may continue until 6 a.m. It features drinking and dancing, and raises money for the bereaved family.

A good time was the goal at the 2012 memorial service for Helen Gurley Brown, former editor-in-chief of *Cosmopolitan* magazine (and creator of "The Cosmo Girl"). The venue was Alice Tully Hall at Lincoln Center, where the fare was chocolate chip cookies and champagne. Attendees wore colorful clothes and Broadway stars performed. Services for composer Marvin Hamlisch (1944–2012) were held at the Metropolitan Museum of Art, where the menu featured lollipops.

54. What's involved in arranging a live-streamed funeral and what should I know about it?

Live streaming allows people who can't attend a funeral to "be there." Viewers log in and watch remotely. All they need is an

Internet connection. They can also invite relatives and friends for company if they wish.

A funeral home, church, or other place of worship can mount cameras to broadcast or live stream a funeral. Broadcasting is certainly done when public figures and celebrities die (ranging from Princess Diana to Aretha Franklin and Pope John Paul II). A live stream can be a blessing to the bereaved, especially when there's an unexpected death and the deceased's religion requires a fast funeral. Some people can't travel on short notice or are ill or too frail to make the trip. In addition, families are often scattered, and the need to attend can be a burden. The bereaved may be able to watch later on, as well.

One survey found that the attitude toward streaming varies according to age. One-third of respondents aged eighteen to thirty-four felt comfortable watching a funeral at home instead of attending in person, whereas 23 percent in the thirty-five to fifty-four age group felt this way. Incidentally, watching the live stream can be a less frightening way to introduce a child to the idea of a funeral.

In business situations, however, watching a funeral on your couch in the den can be misguided. You don't want to be a "no show" when the boss's mother dies, for example, and everyone else at the company attends in person.

55. What exactly is cremation?

According to the Cremation Association of North America, "Cremation is the mechanical, thermal, or other dissolution process that reduces human remains to bone fragments." The fragments are called cremated remains, or cremains for short. The burning of a body into ashes actually goes back to the Stone Age and has origins in Europe. However, European Christians believed in whole body burial, though the black plague compelled the Christians to use cremation so as to prevent the scourge from spreading. In the United States today, the body is cremated in a container, and the bereaved can dispose of the ashes in several ways.

An urn is often used to store the ashes. A wide variety of materials and shapes is available in a range of prices. The size of an urn counts, depending on how it will be used, where it will be placed, and the height/weight of the deceased. For example, will the urn be displayed at home or in a columbarium—or buried? In the latter case (and if you're going to scatter the ashes), an inexpensive urn is fine. You might want a classier model if the urn will be prominently displayed above the fireplace. Urns can be made of crystal, glass, ceramic, wood, metal, or biodegradable materials.

Ashes can also be converted into cremation jewelry, such as rings, pendants, bracelets, earrings—even diamonds. According to The Cremation Institute, diamonds are made from carbon contained in the deceased's ashes and hair. You can choose stones from a variety of shapes, such as brilliant or radiant cut, as well as sizes and colors. Several companies sell such items online.

You can witness a cremation if you wish, although some crematoriums ban it. You may want to scatter the ashes or bury them in a coffin in a cemetery. (If you don't want to buy a casket, you can rent one to use just for the viewing and/or funeral service.) Or you can put the cremains in an urn that is placed in a columbarium (a vault or other structure with niches in the walls to hold them). You can visit the niche the same way you would visit a grave.

Cremation: Key Terms

- **Cremation container** or **alternative container**. The body is transported to the crematory in this container, and the body may or may not be cremated in it.
- Cremation container or **urn vault**. If the ashes are buried, the cemetery's rules and requirements about the container must be observed. For example, an urn isn't (or may not be) just buried. Outer material such as concrete may be needed to protect the urn from the elements.
- A new idea is **alkaline hydrolysis** (water cremation), which involves liquefying a body without releasing carbon dioxide into the air. Hydrolysis costs about the same as flame cremation, but so far it is legal in less than one-third of states.
- **Urn garden**. A specific area in a cemetery dedicated for cremains. Places can be marked with a memorial marker.

56. Who is most likely to choose cremation, and what is *direct cremation?*

According to the Cremation Association of North America, research shows that the size of our mobile population has increased. Result: Some people, such as retirees who often move south or west and Americans who love world travel, are less interested in permanent cemetery plots. Cremation fits their lifestyle and is cheaper. There are no cemetery fees if you scatter ashes to the wind. A funeral or memorial service can be skipped altogether, not to mention a hearse and extras such as vigils and visitations. In addition, religious objections to cremation are diminishing, which helps make this a viable option for many individuals.

Direct cremation is a cremation that is unaccompanied by a viewing, visitation, or formal services of any kind. There is no expensive gathering of people—and no fees for clerical services, either.

57. What should I know about buying a niche in a columbarium?

Niches are receptacles (often of varying sizes) in a columbarium, a structure that contains the ashes of the deceased, which are usually in an urn or other container. Smaller niches, which are the least expensive, can hold the cremains of one person. Larger ones can hold the ashes of two individuals or more. If the thought of burial is the stuff of your nightmares, columbariums are one way to go. They are also better for the environment.

The columbarium can be a wall in a cemetery or other location. It also can be built into a church wall. Niches generally cost anywhere from $700 and up for a single to $3,000 for two or more. At one church, for example, a niche for one is $1,500. In this case, church members get a $300 discount. Freestanding niches can hold two urns. Cremation expenses are extra. Flowers may be placed in a vase at the niche. Incidentally, you can resell an unwanted burial plot fairly easily, but selling a columbarium niche can be much more difficult (or prohibited entirely) if you decide to move away or choose another burial option. However, in some cases a partial refund may be possible. The issue is you don't own the niche, but rather the rights of interment within the niche. For example, if you no longer want your niche in the columbarium at Anchorage Memorial Park Cemetery in Alaska, you can remove the urn and receive a refund of 75 percent of the original price, not including the costs of the marker and perpetual care.

58. Can I scatter my brother's ashes in the backyard?
Maybe. It depends. It's probably okay if you own the property. If not, you need the permission of the legal owner. On the other hand, permits may be required to scatter ashes in public places, such as a park or lake. The legalities can vary from state to state, so expect to do your homework.

In Colorado, for example, you can scatter ashes on your own private property, but you'd better get permission if you want to do it on land owned by others. You can apply for a permit to scatter ashes in Colorado's Rocky Mountain National Park. (The same goes for many other national parks in other states.) In many cemeteries, you can scatter ashes in gardens reserved for that purpose. A plaque memorializes the scattering.

The federal Clean Water Act mandates that ashes should be scattered at sea at least three nautical miles from land. Dispose of the container separately if it will not decompose easily. Scattering at beaches or wading pools by the sea are prohibited by the Environmental Protection Agency (EPA), as detailed on their website. How about dropping ashes from a plane? Because cremains aren't considered hazardous, it should be okay to do so. Just don't throw out the container—federal aviation laws ban dropping items that might harm people or property. These days you can also scatter ashes with drones, which will often take photos, too.

59. What is "wildcat scattering of ashes"?

The term refers to illegal scattering, that is, without permits and/or permission. Although scattering of human ashes is not a health or environmental threat, it does require an "okay" in many cases. It may or may not violate a health code.

However, the bereaved can come up with unconventional ideas these days. For example, during halftime at a Philadelphia Eagles football game, a fan scattered his mother's ashes at the side of the field. And he paid for it—with a fine and the performance of community service.

A man once tossed ashes (supposedly of his mentor) into the orchestra pit at the Metropolitan Opera during intermission. Although convenience may govern the choice of scattering locales, there's often a connection with meaning. It makes sense to scatter the ashes of a deep-sea fisherman or a retired sailor in the ocean. Other bodies of water, such as a lake or a bay may be used, as well.

But do check out the legalities. Many companies have been created to help folks obey the laws. According to the Neptune Society, a national provider of cremation services, state laws vary, and federal law may prevail in scattering over water. As noted in Question 58 above, the federal Clean Water Act decrees that cremains be scattered a minimum of three nautical miles from land. Again, to scatter on private land, you usually need the owner's permission.

On the other hand, the Catholic Church's attitude is that

human ashes should be buried in a cemetery or another sacred place, such as a columbarium. No urns on the fireplace or burials at sea allowed.

60. What is a mausoleum?

It's a stately tomb. The term originates from the tomb of Mausolus, ruler of Caria, in Asia Minor, which was built between 353 and 351 BC, according to the *Encyclopedia Britannica*. The monumental tomb was one of the Seven Wonders of the World. Mausoleums today, although often stately and dignified, are usually above-ground buildings that house a body in a casket. Private mausoleums in cemeteries are built specifically for a single family. Alternatively, more than one family can share a mausoleum to reduce costs.

Cremains can also be entombed in a mausoleum crypt, although the cost is higher than in a columbarium.

61. What is a graveside funeral?

The funeral service is held outdoors at the site of the grave (where chairs are set out for attendees). A graveside funeral is much less expensive (and briefer) than one in a church or funeral home. Graveside funerals may appeal to bereaved who have no religious affiliation—and may also be preferred when only a small number of people will attend. The funeral is simple; there is no music, no pallbearers. However, there may be a eulogy. The arrangement can also work well for cremains being buried.

A graveside service can also follow a traditional funeral, although a smaller number of people will attend.

62. What exactly is a "green funeral" and a "green burial"—and why choose one?

A green funeral is an environmentally friendly way to prepare and bury the dead. All materials must be biodegradable, including the casket, shroud, or urn (in cases of cremation).

Results of a 2017 survey by the National Funeral Directors Association found 53.8 percent of respondents showed interest in protecting the environment via green funerals, which could include biodegradable caskets, formaldehyde-free embalming, recycled paper products, and more. In a survey conducted by funeralOne, a consulting firm that works with the funeral industry, 74 percent of responding families said they did not want a traditional funeral.

Increasing numbers of cemeteries may offer a specially designed "green burial area" or columbarium space, each with its own requirements. The nonprofit Green Burial Council

(GBC), an independent tax-exempt nonprofit organization, certifies "green" cemeteries that care for the dead with minimal environmental impact. This method aids in conserving natural resources, reducing carbon emissions, restoring and/or preserving habitat, and protecting worker health. For example, embalming is discouraged or formaldehyde-free embalming fluids are now being used in place of carcinogenic chemical forms. Caskets made of wood or other biodegradable materials are used. Types, sizes, and visibility of memorial markers must preserve the natural landscape. According to the Pennsylvania Historical and Museum Commission, environmentally sustainable burials are a way to help preserve the earth. Many funeral homes offer green burial services as interest in them has grown.

63. How do I handle disagreements between family members on funeral, memorial service, or other details? My siblings disagree on how much to spend on a casket for our mom and where to bury the body. We all live in different parts of the country.

A large percentage of those who ask for my advice want help dealing with such differences, even when the death has been expected. Some cases involve a matter of perspective. But too often a death becomes the scene of sibling rivalries as issues of control play out. Often one wants to be told "I'm right."

I know of instances where family members have stopped talking to each other over issues such as what to say or omit in a eulogy or obituary. You may ask the funeral director to referee—or, if that doesn't work, there's always the option of hiring a mediator. One question to ask yourselves is, "Would the deceased have wanted arguments over this?" This just isn't the time for acrimony.

Other issues that cause trouble may include: Where do you bury the deceased? Will the deceased be buried with the first, second, or maybe third spouse or partner? Or do you deposit the ashes in one urn (or Mason jar)? Or do you divvy them up among survivors? And which bereaved makes the decision?

64. Can I limit attendees without alienating anyone?

Some bereaved families want to bask in the glow of a crowded funeral. They want to see rows and rows of people paying respects to the deceased and the survivors, because to them it represents a fitting tribute. The numbers validate the regard in which they are held—and these numbers elevate the occasion. For some, it can be a comfort to walk down the aisle and see people they never expected to see, people who went out of their way to attend.

In contrast, others want privacy—to be surrounded only by

those near and dear (or who were very close to the deceased). Others might consider a huge turnout akin to a circus.

If you wish to limit the attendance, you can omit any mention of time, location, and other details in the obituary. It's a signal that only people who have been personally invited by the bereaved should attend. Or the obit may say explicitly, "Services will be private for the family." Most people will understand and not take it personally.

65. When the deceased is not being cremated and the casket will be open at the funeral, how do the bereaved choose the clothing for the body? What are the criteria?

If the family is lucky, the decision will have been made by the bereaved in advance.

If not, you might consult with the funeral home or pick clothing you believe the deceased would have wanted for the occasion. For example, after the Queen of Soul, Aretha Franklin, died, her family scheduled three different viewings in Detroit, before the funeral. At the first viewing, at the Charles H. Wright Museum of African American History, her open gold-plated casket was surrounded by cascades of pink, yellow, and lavender roses. She wore a flaming red dress and Christian Louboutin red stiletto heels to mark her honorary membership in Delta Sigma Theta sorority. At a second viewing the next day, she wore a powder blue dress and matching shoes in a bronze casket. At the third and last viewing, at the New Bethel Baptist Church, she wore rose gold. A lineup of pink Cadillacs was part of her funeral procession to the megachurch Greater Grace Temple, which holds 4,000 people.

Families that want to capture the personality of the deceased can choose an outfit that the deceased would have liked and that reflects the person. I know of one man who was buried in his baseball cap. The fact is, people can be buried with anything they might have wanted, such as photos or a favorite piece of jewelry. For less than grand events, families can pick clothing from the deceased's closet or buy something new.

66. What's a "funeral celebrant"?

Let me introduce you to a new category in funeral options, which has emerged in the United States mainly because 20 percent of Americans are now unaffiliated with any religion. According to the Celebrant Foundation & Institute (CFI) in Montclair, New Jersey, a funeral celebrant is a qualified, nonclergy individual who works with a family to make a funeral memorable. Use of celebrants is especially common in Australia, where more than 60 percent of funerals involve celebrants, who can even deliver a eulogy if family members or friends are too distraught to do it themselves. Funeral celebrants are one category of "life cycle celebrants," which also includes celebrants for weddings and other occasions. The celebrant may or may not work with a funeral director. Funeral celebrants certified by CFI are available in most states of the United States, Canada, Mexico, and several other countries. The National Funeral Directors Association now offers celebrant training.

A funeral celebrant may charge a flat fee or an hourly rate. The bill may run a few hundred dollars or more, depending on the services. Some celebrants specialize in alternative or "themed" services. Others offer more traditional services. An increasing number of people want a less religious or a nonreligious humanist funeral today, and this is a way to do it.

67. What are the criteria for selecting eulogy speakers?

Suitable choices include friends of the deceased, close relatives, and long-time business or professional associates (such as a boss who was like a mother). Realize, however, that some people may turn down the honor because they're terrified at the thought of public speaking or are too overwrought with grief to take the podium. So keep some possible replacements in mind. If there is more than one eulogy, you may want to ask the speakers to coordinate what they're saying to avoid repeating the same old story.

It used to be that women rarely gave eulogies, but times are changing. At the last memorial service I attended—for a friend—several women (including me) spoke.

68. How should I thank the pallbearers? Is a note okay, or should I give each some kind of gift (or even money)?

Neither a gift nor money is necessary. However, do send a thoughtful note of appreciation. You might consider words such as, "You were my sister's best friend. She respected and admired you, as do all of us. Thank you for all your kindnesses to her throughout her life and especially during her long illness."

69. Should I consider a home funeral? What are the advantages?

Funerals used to be held at home all the time. But that changed with the Civil War, when bodies were shipped home and embalming became popular. Today, the growth of nonprofit funeral home groups and green cemeteries suggest new interest in home funerals. Bodies can also be buried in land adjacent to (or in back of) the family home in many cases. This choice is also appealing because home funerals are cheaper than other venues. They're also legal in every state.

Because we whisper about death in our society, some people believe a home funeral makes the death easier to bear and process. Many find it healing, meaningful, and therapeutic. A funeral celebrant can be helpful here, too (see Question 66: "What's a 'funeral celebrant'?" on page 96). Funeral homes will often work with the family, as well. Many states don't have preservation time requirements for the body. Freezer packs are sometimes used instead of embalming. If you don't embalm, the body decomposes as nature intended. Embalming is all about preserving the deceased's appearance, but the process uses harsh chemicals to do so.

According to the Green Burial Council (GBC), most states allow home funerals with or without the assistance of a licensed funeral director. Only eight states require a funeral director to handle preparation of the body and otherwise supervise a home funeral.

Home burials are allowed in many counties, although regulations vary, according to the GBC. For more resources on home funerals, contact the National Home Funeral Alliance (homefuneralalliance.org) and the Funeral Consumers Alliance (funerals.org).

70.

How do I host a memorial service at home? What's involved?

A home memorial service is much easier than a funeral because the actual body won't be present. The deceased has already been buried elsewhere or has been cremated.

When her close colleague died, a friend of mine teamed up with the bereaved husband to plan a home memorial gathering of friends and family. See the accompanying box for questions to ask when considering a home memorial service.

It's important to check out alternatives to a home memorial. In this case, the bereaved husband researched restaurants that rented private rooms or spaces for events large or small. He decided not to rent a space for a few reasons: They seemed impersonal because they were unfamiliar, and they were expensive. In addition, the restaurants usually required attendees to exit the premises at a specific time. The flexibility and warmth of a home venue won out.

Questions to Ask Yourself When Planning a Memorial at Home

- How many people will you invite? The answer will determine the size of the space required and whether it's possible to handle the number of attendees at home (yours or someone else's) or if the number requires that you rent a restaurant or other space. A home event requires a spacious area where people can mingle comfortably and enough places for seating.

- Who will share the tasks? Will you assemble a group of relatives and/or friends to do it together or will you tackle the job yourself? Some of us throw up our hands at one guest for dinner. Others feel very comfortable serving (and even cooking for) a crowd. Who will email invitations and/or ask people whether they wish to speak? Who will handle food and drinks? You can serve wine or light refreshments or you can put out a full buffet of food you made yourself (or was contributed by others) or you can have the whole thing catered. A very casual spread can use paper plates and plastic glasses and cutlery. When planning, keep in mind whether or not you will need babysitting help for your (or guests') children.
- How will you create a program? Yes, people will mingle, but organization counts. You need a host or hostess, and you need someone to play the role of master of ceremonies.
- As for letting people know about the event, you can use social media like Facebook to create a memorial page where friends and family anywhere in the country (or the world) can receive details and information. Ask attendees in advance for suggestions and stories. Decide on the order of speakers (and confer with others for advice, if needed). It's probably wise to mention a word limit to ensure someone doesn't wind up monopolizing the time. And ask only a select group of people to speak so it doesn't take three hours to hear everyone.
- How will you plan the cleanup? Are you going to do it yourself or will you ask for a volunteer crew? Or will you call a cleaning service?
- What's your budget? Can you afford to hire a bartender and/or server if you wish to go the extra mile? Everyone's budget is different. Will you borrow chairs or rent them? How about one or more tables? Or a coat rack?
- Who will handle decorations? The latter can include a display of family photos, snapshots, flowers, and the like.

71.

How do you send the body home when a loved one dies overseas—and how much does it cost?

More Americans die overseas than we imagine. One man I heard of had a heart attack while bicycle riding on a vacation with his family in Sicily. Another died working out on a treadmill in a Paris hotel. Accidents do occur. We always suppose they happen to other people, but sometimes it's us or a loved one—leaving next of kin to cope with not only the loss, but also with the decisions, arrangements, red tape, and expense involved in "repatriation of remains" to the United States. The to-do list includes navigating local laws, obtaining required permits, and handling other paperwork in the country of death—plus dealing with US regulations for accepting the body or cremains and the containers that hold them.

Be aware that the Bureau of Consular Affairs of the US Department of State aids families of American citizens who need transport help. In 2017 the Bureau assisted the families of 11,274 US citizens who died overseas. The Bureau locates next of kin and educates them on their options, such as local burial in the foreign country. You, however, must pay the cost of making it happen, such as preparation of the body and shipping. For example, embalming is expensive, although most next-of-kin want it, according to the National Funeral Directors Association. Delta Cargo, United Airlines, Southwest Cargo, and American Airlines offer services to help families transport human remains in these circumstances, including in the United States.

For an overview on dealing with a death abroad, see the website travel.state.gov. The State Department's Overseas Citizen Services operates a 24-hours-a-day hotline at 202-624-5225. Or you can delegate the job to a funeral home that specializes in arranging international funeral transportation—and is savvy about minimizing hassles and unnecessary costs. Whatever you decide, you'll find that cremation before shipment is the easiest and cheapest way to go. What about death on a cruise ship? Large ships have morgues on board and can usually carry the body to a port equipped to send it home.

Travel Insurance: Evacuation and Repatriation

Although many people buy travel insurance to defray unexpected costs due to illness or injury, they may be surprised to find that the policy might not cover the shipment of the remains home when the policyholder dies. Rules, regulations, bureaucracy, legal details, and other red tape abound in the country of death. In addition, the remains will not be accepted in the United States unless a long list of requirements are followed. Check out bereavement fares if you want to accompany the body. It's a complicated and expensive process, and buying travel insurance that covers these specific costs is worth considering.

According to travel insurance expert Damian Tysdal, most travel insurance plans that offer evacuation coverage for illness or injury also include repatriation. The term is often listed as "Evacuation and Repatriation." If it's a trip insurance package plan, the policy cost is based on the cost of the trip, the traveler's age, and travel dates. For a standalone travel medical plan, the cost is based on the traveler's age and trip length

If you plan to engage in potentially dangerous activities such as mountain climbing, scuba diving, or zip lining (an extreme sport that involves zipping through platforms on a series of cables), you should upgrade the plan to include coverage for hazardous sports.

72. What's the difference between a coffin and a casket? Can they be rented?

A coffin is tapered at the head and foot and wide at the shoulders. A casket, usually higher quality in materials and workmanship than a coffin, is rectangular. Rental is possible at many funeral homes. Rentals make sense, as anyone who has shopped for a casket in recent years is well aware. According to *Forbes*, there's a 289 percent markup on caskets from wholesale to retail. Rental allows families to display the bereaved in a handsome coffin for a viewing or visitation. The body is actually in a plain wooden box inside the coffin. The box is what is buried at the cemetery. The same can be done if the body will be cremated after the funeral.

73. I heard that you can buy a casket or an urn for ashes at both Costco and Walmart. Is that really true? Also, what's an "overnight casket"?

Hard as it may be to believe, it is indeed true that these meccas for food, household and medicine cabinet supplies, clothing, you name it, also sell products for funeral needs. And you can get caskets from other online retailers, including Amazon. They offer a variety of shapes, brands, sizes, colors, and prices. Caskets are generally made of wood, metal, or stainless steel.

Pet urns are available in bronze and other materials. Some are made of recycled material. Adult urns can be purchased, too.

An overnight casket is one that is shipped to you by the next day, sometimes with free delivery.

74. I've heard that a casket can explode. Is that true?

Yes indeed. "Protective" or "sealer" caskets, which sell for big bucks, come with the promise to prevent air and moisture from entering the casket. Without these elements, the body will not deteriorate in above-ground burials in mausoleums. However, the casket can explode, due to a buildup of methane gas inside.

75. Are caskets for severely obese people more expensive?

Yes. Surprising issues can turn up in funeral planning. Caskets are often the most expensive items in funerals, even if the deceased is skinny. Folks who are severely overweight and want to be buried are going to pay an extra premium for the coffin.

76.

How can I crowdfund a funeral or memorial service—and why is it so popular these days?

Back in the 1800s, English author Samuel Butler said, "It costs a lot of money to die comfortably." Butler had no idea how the cost would skyrocket in the twenty-first century. According to the 2018 statistics from the National Funeral Directors Association, the median cost of a funeral with viewing and burial is $8,755. For cremation and viewing, the median cost is $6,260. No wonder home funerals, cremation, and crowdfunding are new trends. (Note that crowdfunding aims to raise small amounts of money from many people, as opposed to crowdsourcing where the sky is the limit, and startups, among others, can seek financing in the millions for huge projects.)

Why do people do it? Because catastrophes seem to lurk everywhere today—fires, floods, and more—and economic need is all around us. A young father dies suddenly in an accident. A long-ill grandmother dies, leaving her struggling family to pay medical, memorial service, and cremation fees. A family is wiped out in a fire, leaving relatives not only with intense grief but also with the funeral bill. Many deceased don't have life insurance or estates to cover the costs.

Crowdfunding Online

Among the largest crowdfunding sites is GoFundMe (gofundme
.com), which found that 13 percent of its crowdfunding was for
funeral and other memorial expenses. The site runs over 125,000
memorial campaigns a year and people have raised over $330
million for such purposes. There is an age gap in usage. A recent
study by the Funeral and Memorial Information Council (FAMIC)
found that younger adults, aged twenty to thirty-nine, are more
likely (17 percent) than older people (4 percent) to use Internet crowdfunding to raise money for funeral or other memorial
costs. Crowdfunding sites' fees vary and are subject to change.
Essentially, none are free, although the term "free" may be used
at times.

For the bereaved, crowdfunding is a way to raise money
for these expenses without putting themselves or others in
an uncomfortable financial position. Crowdfunding is also a
relief for people who want to help the bereaved, but don't know
what to do. Family, friends, and even strangers contribute—
and sometimes the proceeds greatly top the projected goal.
However, crowdfunding can have a downside. Not every campaign raises the target amount, and some families can wind
up with a fraction of their goal. What's more, family members
and friends may resent being asked directly to chip in for a
funeral when they feel no better off (or even less well off) than
the bereaved.

An online crowdfunding campaign is not the only way

the bereaved can get help in defraying costs. Local churches, synagogues, and other places of worship may have money set aside for such crises. I know of one that even provides a burial plot for the needy. In some cases, family or friends of the deceased may put "donation jars" for a funeral in local public places, such as fast food restaurants, gas stations, and stores to raise money for a funeral in the community. Unfortunately, not all such efforts are legitimate. I know of a scammer who stole a woman's photograph from Facebook and used it with a stranger's name on donation jars that were placed in retail locations. Fortunately, the ruse was discovered before the money was collected, but such scams are not uncommon.

The government provides burial benefits for veterans; these benefits vary depending on whether the death is service related or not. Visit the US Department of Veterans Affairs website for information (benefits.va.gov/benefits).

77. What's a "virtual memorial"?

Virtual memorials are commemorative websites that can host thousands of family or individual pages where the bereaved can celebrate a lost loved one. Younger people are likelier to create one and visit one. Survivors can post photos and share memories of the deceased. Poetry, eulogies, and even music may be included, as well, plus funeral information. Sites such as Legacy.com might include a guest book and offer templates to help the bereaved set up the memorial. Prices vary, and some virtual websites are free for basic services but charge for extras. Others might charge a one-time fee (such as $20 or $55 or more). Note, however, that the memorial pages are not permanent. They may stay online for a year (or less, or more).

I saw one virtual memorial for a teenager that received over 13,000 visits. It included a slide show, photo album, and guest book. Another for an adult received 800 visits. It varies.

78. What is a funeral or memorial society or co-op? The first memorial society in the United States was founded in 1938 to help the bereaved reduce funeral home and burial costs. In the nineteenth century, European immigrants to the United States started burial societies. The idea was to have an affordable funeral. It's estimated that more than 200 such societies operated in the United States. In 1985 the People's Memorial Association, based in Seattle, Washington, had over 40,000 members. This association is affiliated with the Funeral Consumers Alliance, which is the only national consumer organization that advocates for fair funeral practices on behalf of consumers.

People's Memorial Association (peoplesmemorial.org) provides a great example of how membership in such a society can help with costs. For $50 you receive a lifetime membership. If you're a member, you would receive a roughly 10 percent to 15 percent reduction in the price of services like cremation or a direct burial with a gravesite service. Prices do go up, but they're reasonable.

Every state has an affiliate of the Funeral Consumers Alliance (funerals.org). Visit the website for state-by-state information about funeral and memorial societies.

79. How much should I expect to pay for an honorarium for a funeral?

In the United States, most churches don't charge for the funeral service of a member, but donations may be common. Nonmembers may pay a rental fee. An honorarium might run from $150 to $300 or more, depending on the location and congregation. Many people make a donation to the priest for celebrating a funeral. But it is not required. However, organists and church musicians should be paid. At one Jewish memorial service I know of, the honorarium was $600. If in doubt, ask the funeral director about what's appropriate. (It is not acceptable to ask a clergyman about the fee.) There may be a surcharge for services at night or on weekends.

To head off surprises and disagreements after the funeral,

it's a smart idea to call the place of worship and ask about its policies. Everyone is fragile and on edge before, during, and after a funeral. Why run the risk of needless upset at an already difficult time?

Churches: Who Covers the Cost?

An online poll conducted in Canada by the publication *Christian Courier* found memorial services (but not necessarily funerals) were free to members at 82 percent of surveyed churches, although voluntary contributions were acceptable at some churches. In the same survey, 18 percent of churches charged rent for use of the premises, which might be used to cover cleaning services. Other interesting stats included:

- 12 percent of churches paid for some funeral food.
- In 16 percent of cases, members donated all the food.
- In 26 percent of cases, half of the food involved donations and half was provided by the bereaved family.
- In 46 percent of cases, the family paid the full tab.
- 30 percent of churches charged no pastor honorarium.

---

80. What work does a minister perform for a funeral?

There's a lot involved, including family visits, preparation of the liturgy and meditations, and conducting the service itself. This can require anywhere from ten to fifteen hours of work or more, depending on the situation.

81.
Should I place a death notice or an obituary? What's the difference?

The word *obit* is Latin for "he or she died," and published death notices have been called obituaries since the 1700s. Today the general public often uses the terms *obituary* and *death notice* interchangeably. However, there is a difference, officially. A death notice is a paid announcement of someone's death (basically a classified ad) that includes information on the funeral or memorial service and mentions where to send donations in memory of the deceased. The notice usually lists immediate survivors, and may or may not include biographical information and/or a photo of the deceased. Newspapers charge by the inch or by the line. The notice can run as long (and for as many days) as the family wishes (and is willing to pay for). Death notices can be surprisingly expensive. For example, a standard short notice in the *Baltimore Sun* might run $350 for one day and hit $800 or $900 if it's twice the length. Newspapers in big cities charge as much as $100 or more per inch, not including an extra fee for a photo.

In contrast, an obituary in a large newspaper is free to the bereaved and is written by the newspaper staff. The paper decides who is newsworthy enough to qualify. For example, the *Baltimore Sun* focuses on people visible in Baltimore, such the CEO of a local company or the coach of a team. The newspaper decides if, when, and for how long it will run. Larger circulation newspapers, such as the *New York Times* and *Washington Post* may run "official obituaries" that draw from their archives of famous figures in the arts, sciences, politics, law, business, or education.

There is no requirement to write and place an obituary (death notice). In my own family, obituaries were unheard of until recent decades and were considered only for the rich and famous. But times have changed. A study of 1,000 people by Legacy.com found 88 percent of respondents said they would run a paid newspaper obituary.

Today, many funeral homes have their own websites where families can post an obituary for a loved one. The staff will help families compose the obit, if desired. Some obits tell us of the human spirit, others of simple lives, others of achievements and accomplishments. Obituaries are often ripe with irony. One obit, written by the newspaper staff, announced the accidental death of a noted mountain climber—who fell down the stairs at home.

In order to publish an obituary, a death certificate must be filed with a state office of vital statistics. Obituaries have other uses beyond just describing the deceased. For example, an obit can say, "A memorial service will be held next spring." People who receive a call or some kind of announcement beforehand know they are invited. If they don't receive this notice, they're not on the list.

In some cases, in addition to the obituary placed by the bereaved, notices may be run by other relatives or friends, employers, business and professional connections or associations, and/or cultural or charitable institutions or organizations that benefited from the deceased's support.

82. What's an online obituary and how does it work?

Some newspapers, especially large ones, now publish obituaries online. The online versions can run 20 or 30 percent less than the print versions. For example, you can run an online death notice in the *New York Times* for less than $100. (The print version would cost five times as much). It will be permanently available in the paper's online obit section. There are also commercial websites, such as Legacy.com, where you can run an obituary. Most funeral homes have their own websites where families can run obituaries free of charge.

Another option: Run just a few lines in the newspaper that direct readers to a website for a full-length obituary, as in "Vivian Smith died at home in Cincinnati on May 2, 2018. For a complete obituary, visit (website of funeral home or another website)."

83. How do I write an obituary? Can I ask someone else to write it? How long should it be?

The basics of an obituary comprise essential facts: name of deceased, age or date of birth, date of death, cause of death, occupation, education, career and/or other accomplishments, and notable talents, using phrases such as "a devoted amateur boxer" or "a ceramicist in his spare time," or "a menace on the tennis court." A list of survivors follows, as well as funeral or memorial service details and information on the wake or vigil or shiva, if they are to be held.

The obituary you write for someone may be different from the obituary another person might write. We're different people, after all, and we see and appreciate different qualities and have different memories. This is why it's smart to confer with others when you write an obituary. Their input will help you round it out. Seek help if you don't feel up to the task. I know of a newly widowed woman who was far too shell-shocked to write an obituary for her husband. Her niece volunteered to compose it. After consulting with the widow's grown children, the niece wrote a draft and ran it past the bereaved. Not everyone has such a person handy, of course, but help is out there.

The obituary departments of newspapers will help you write a death notice, if you ask.

Many websites, including Legacy.com, offer templates for obituaries. You fill in a form online, providing necessary facts and information. Legacy.com can also connect you with your local newspaper.

You can personalize as much (or as little) as you wish. For color, you can quote the deceased, as in "She always told her grandchildren to 'Dream big.'" You can dig further and talk to the deceased's coworkers/colleagues for their "take." Look for the little things that humanize the deceased. These details can ennoble ordinary people. For example, "He'll always be remembered with a cigar in his mouth."

I recall one obit that spoke of the deceased "going steady with his spouse at sixteen." It was such a simple detail, yet so humanizing and revealing. Ask yourself, "What was unique about this person?" Perhaps the individual collected antique maps or would walk a mile for a milkshake or was an authority on pizza crusts or acted as travel guru for the entire family. The idea is to portray the essence of the person. Instead of saying something generic like, "He was the most generous person I ever knew," you might put it this way: "He literally gave me the shirt off his back when I admired it."

How far you go is up to you. I've read obituaries that mention the deceased's struggles with alcoholism and attendance at AA meetings. Today, an obit may even mention opioid addiction as the cause of death, in a decision by the family to try to help others.

Many obits conclude with a line or two about suggested donations. The wording may be something like, "The family requests that any contributions in memory of _____ be made to (name of charity, institution, or other worthy cause)." On the other hand, I've recently seen statements like, "Contributions may be made to the charity of your choice."

Know how much you want to spend to determine your word count. I recently saw a full-page obituary, run by the bereaved, in the main section of a major newspaper. However, few of us can afford (or would wish to run) such an announcement.

84.

What should I know about choosing an obit photo for my mother? I've seen photos of beautiful young women and strong attractive young men at the top of obits for ninety-year-olds. In my opinion, it's silly.

Including a photo of the deceased in an obit involves added expense, and it's up to you whether to use one. The deceased may also have left instructions about using a particular preferred photo. I personally hope my family will choose a flattering photo taken in recent years before my death. The deceased may have specifically requested a "youthful" picture from decades ago, because they want to be remembered at the peak of their good looks.

85.

Which survivors should be mentioned in an obituary and how can I set priorities? My father, who has children and grandchildren from two marriages, is in hospice and I have to start planning.

Ah, yes. Obits used to be simple in the old days. Today, they can become battlegrounds for long simmering resentments and family feuds. It's not only a question of who you do or don't mention in cases of blended or estranged families, it may also be a question of who gets listed first when naming survivors. (The term *survivor* can be open to wide interpretation and include ex-mothers-in-law, cousins of ex's, and a long list of other possibilities.) It can cost a bundle if you mention everybody in a paid obituary in cases of multiple marriages. You're charged by the line and it can get expensive if you name the twelve grandchildren rather than say, "and twelve loving grandchildren."

One possibility is to include more names in a free obituary and stick to the essentials in the paid obituary. Be prepared, however. Some people feel crushed when omitted from the obituary of a loved one. Other people will never be satisfied and may feel left out no matter what you do. It's really important to list people, but there are budget considerations, too. Just remember that the point is not to play out rivalries (sibling and otherwise) or settle scores with other bereaved, but to memorialize and mourn the deceased.

86. Do I have to mention cause of death in an obituary?

No. However, if you decide to mention the cause of death, you can be discreet with respect to the details. Some mentions I've seen include: "Died in his sleep"; "Died in a nursing home"; "The cause of death was pneumonia"; "Died from injuries in a traffic accident"; "Lost her struggle with multiple illnesses"; "Died after a courageous battle with colon cancer"; and "Had a stroke after jogging in the park."

If the obituary was written by the newspaper staff, the wording might be something like, "Her daughter said the cause of death was a heart attack." Mentions of suicide are tricky. This may be expressed with a phrase like, "She suffered from depression for years."

87. I've seen classified In Memoriams on the obituary page that do not refer to a recent death, but instead mark the anniversary of a death. Or it may simply say something like, "I miss you, Dad," or include poetry. What are these?

These are commemorative announcements. They may mark a specific anniversary of the death (one year, ten years, and so forth), or the birthday of the deceased, or a family event (such as a birth or a graduation or wedding) that brings to mind the deceased and stirs wishes that the deceased could attend and share the happiness. Or an In Memoriam can be published simply because the bereaved misses the person. A commemorative In Memoriam can be placed by one person or a group (for example: "The Smith Family" or "The Green and Swanson Families" or "The deceased's sibling and sister-in-law").

On Father's Day and Mother's Day, don't be surprised to see a long list of commemorative In Memoriams running in newspaper obituary sections. These commemorations usually express sentiments of love and/or reminisce over the past. Christmas, Thanksgiving, and the New Year are big holidays, too, for these commemorations.

Cheat Sheet: Examples of Wording for "Complicated" Obituaries

Ms. Smith's marriage in 2000 to _____ ended in divorce in 2003. She did not remarry. She is survived by her son, Peter, her brother, Robert, and sister, Kate.

He was predeceased by his first wife, Mary, and is survived by his wife, Inga.

Survivors include her longtime companion, Joseph Ross, two daughters, and four grandchildren.

He is survived by his second wife, Elizabeth, three children from a previous marriage to _____, which ended in divorce, and many grandchildren and greatgrandchildren.

No immediate family members survive.

Prices for these notices vary (and continually change.). For example, at large newspapers, prices for a commemorative In Memoriam might start at anywhere from $25 to about $100.

Incidentally, it's never too late to run an In Memoriam. I recently saw one that commemorated victims of a major plane crash 50 years ago—placed by a survivor of the crash. Another In Memoriam of a few lines honored a deceased on the fiftieth anniversary of the death.

88.

What are acknowledgment cards, and to whom should I send them? I'm overwhelmed at the thought of writing to everyone who attended my aunt's funeral or emailed condolences.

Acknowledgment cards are a type of thank you card sent to people who made donations in memory of the deceased, sent flowers or food, or performed acts of kindness (such as picking up out-of-towners at the airport or walking the dog when you could barely put one foot in front of the other). You don't have to write to people who simply attended the funeral.

You can buy printed acknowledgment cards, and then add a handwritten line or two, saying something like: "Your beautiful plant reminds me every day of your support." Note that it's important to mention what was sent (or done) to personalize your note. Or you can say, "I can't tell you how much your many kindnesses meant to me in the last few weeks."

Personally, I also make it a policy to send acknowledgment cards to those who send me handwritten condolence notes or printed condolence cards with more than just a signature—for instance, a personal message that requires some thought and effort.

89. How late is too late to send acknowledgments? I lost three members of my family last year, but I break down every time I sit down to write. And how do I acknowledge online or email condolences?

It's never too late in a case like yours. You've had multiple losses in a short period of time, which can be devastating. It's very important to take care of yourself; research shows that loss of a significant person in your life puts your health at risk. Bereavement takes an enormous toll on the immune system. Risk of heart attack rises shortly after a death and funeral. Even risk for accidents increases. It is perfectly acceptable to ask a friend or family member to help you with the task. You'll feel a lot less alone and finish faster.

Anyone who writes notes for you can say words to the effect of, "Mary asked me to thank you for all your assistance since Ken's death" or "Our family appreciates your generous donation to the American Cancer Society." As for timing, remember that nobody is checking the calendar for the arrival of your acknowledgment. People understand you're recovering from an enormous shock.

Today, people also express sympathy by email or on the website of a funeral home, newspaper, or family. In responding, one option is to send one email to a list of people, saying something like, "My thanks for your kind words and thoughts at this difficult time." If someone's online condolence was special in some way, you can send an individual acknowledgment via email.

90.

What's a "card of thanks"?

A card of thanks is a paid notice in the newspaper obituary section that expresses gratitude to all who have sent condolences and/or assisted the bereaved during the time of loss, or who have simply "shown up" with their presence and moral support. This can be the place to thank people who attended the funeral, if you wish. For example, someone who volunteers to mow the lawn or sends a cleaning service to the bereaved's home qualify—as do others in the community who pick up the children after school, drop them off at soccer practice, or take them to the movies on a rainy Saturday. The ad can single out individuals by name or not.

By contrast, an acknowledgment card is a more personal, tangible "thank you." It is sent to acknowledge instances of major help that was given at time of need. Cards are also sent to acknowledge received items such as flowers or baskets, as well as donations to charities, institutions, or causes in memory of the deceased.

A card of thanks ad is also useful when you don't know the addresses of some people who made charitable contributions in memory of the deceased. Instead of trying to track them down at a time when you're already overwhelmed, you can include the names in your card of thanks ad. Some charities, such as the American Cancer Society, not only acknowledge the donation to the bereaved but also send along an addressed envelope and thank you card to the bereaved, inscribed with the words, "The kindness expressed by your gift to the American Cancer Society has been received with heartfelt appreciation." A separate small sheet tells the bereaved, "The enclosed card has been provided to express your appreciation for this memorial gift." An outer envelope is addressed to the contributor. All the bereaved has to do is sign the card, perhaps add a handwritten line or two, and mail the card to the contributor.

Planning Ahead

91.
What is "end of life planning" and why does the term keep coming up these days?

End of life planning involves thinking through your attitude toward quality of life issues before death is at the doorstep. For example, do you want to be kept on life support forever if there is no chance of meaningful recovery? It's critical to communicate your wishes to others.

The goal of end of life planning is to talk about and prepare for a meaningful end. A will is an essential part of this planning. However, according to *Forbes*, over half of Americans don't have a will. A "living will" and appointing a health care proxy should be priorities.

A nonprofit organization called Reimagine (letsreimagine .org) hosts the Reimagine End of Life initiative. This initiative challenges Americans to discuss attitudes about quality of life at the end and to reimagine how we prepare for death and live through the final chapter. A week of related events took place in New York in the fall of 2018. Other events will occur in other cities in the future.

92. Can I plan my own funeral?

Yes. Some people plan out every detail. But you don't have to go that far. At the very least, you should consider preparing some plans that are ready to go when needed. These steps will save your family a lot of anxiety and distress at a very difficult time. Interestingly, according to research by the Funeral and Memorial Information Council (FAMIC), 69 percent of people say they prefer to arrange their own funeral or memorial service, but only 17 percent have actually done so.

The late Arizona Senator John McCain, a Navy pilot who spent five and a half years in a North Vietnam prisoner-of-war camp (and refused early release before his comrades were freed), started planning his memorial service well in advance. McCain chose pallbearers and asked luminaries to give eulogies long before he finally succumbed to brain cancer in 2018. He also planned the music: Frank Sinatra singing the classic, "My Way" as the recessional. He chose to be buried at the US Naval Academy in Annapolis, Maryland, so that his final resting place would be among other Navy heroes, from the Civil War to the present.

Writer and filmmaker Nora Ephron planned her own memorial service while she was dying of leukemia, and she filed her notes in a folder tabbed "Exit." Comedienne Joan Rivers orchestrated her own service too. Planning guarantees that you'll get what you want. There's a bonus, as well. You can head off disagreements about funeral details among those you leave behind. You truly have the final word.

Results of a 2017 Consumer Awareness and Preferences Study by the National Funeral Directors Association found that people generally support preplanning, yet don't follow through and do it: It's not a priority or they haven't thought about it or they feel intimidated by the decisions that must be made or they don't want to pay the costs now. In addition, those who do plan ahead typically don't shop around. Only 18.9 percent of preplanners contacted more than one funeral home to compare prices and services. According to the study, 62.5 percent of Americans feel that it's very important to talk to others about funeral plans, yet only 21.4 percent have made prearrangements for themselves. Nontraditional locations are growing in popularity, such as at home or out in nature. In one case the funeral for a lifelong gardener was held near his pepper plants. Personality counts, too. Some people want a very dignified event where funeral attendees dress conservatively and in dark colors. Others want a party atmosphere with jelly beans and printed T-shirts.

Preplanning does require time and effort. You must

contemplate exactly what you want and research the best way to make it happen. This is an emotional experience that involves figuring out exactly how you feel about who and what and why. Issues include varying state laws, how to fund your funeral, how much you want to spend (and on what). If you're going to do it right, this is one time not to "assume" anything. Many of us don't want to face issues of mortality, and shy away from accounting for every little detail for a (hopefully) far-in-the-future event. Planning your own death can be an ordeal. Some people feel very comfortable nailing down every item, but it's okay if you can't handle it. I have a lot of difficulty with it myself. I almost had a nervous breakdown writing a will and doing financial planning, despite expert help. Confession: I haven't written my own obituary yet, probably because I'm just not ready yet to confront my own illusions about mortality and contemplate my own demise.

93. What's a "living funeral" and why do some people want one?

Also known as a "predeath funeral," this type of event is positive, often joyous, and is held while a dying person is still alive. We think of "celebrations of life" as funerals or memorial services that pay tribute to a deceased. But this version allows the dying to witness and participate in the proceedings—and plan it along with loved ones.

The living funeral can be run by you and/or your family and friends, and can range from a simple gathering in your living room or backyard to a party in a hospice, a community center, restaurant, or place of worship. Food can be included or not. The event can be religious or not. It's an opportunity to hear what your near and dear want you to know—and to share memories and tell life stories, passing them on to future generations. Some feel it may be a way to heal long-standing rifts, as well. To learn more, Denise Carson, a columnist for the *Orange County Register*, discusses the use of living funerals for hospice patients in her book, *Parting Ways*.

The idea of celebrating life is a relatively new phenomenon in the West. The best-selling book *Tuesdays with Morrie: An Old Man, a Young Man, and Life's Greatest Lesson* by Mitch Albom, published in 1997, portrayed a living funeral. Many point to the book as the starting place for this trend. However, the Japanese have been using such events since the 1990s, pushed by the elderly themselves who were concerned with the burdens they placed on their children.

Not all people welcome the idea of a living funeral and may feel uncomfortable attending one. Others may find it impossible to be honest with the about-to-die person in such a setting. There are those who believe it's self-centered and/or a bid for compliments. Yet there's no question a living funeral can be a big money saver.

At a funeral expo held in Tokyo, people who wanted to rehearse their funerals could try out "death" by lying in coffins and write notes with detailed funeral instructions for their families.

94. What's the difference between "pre-need" funeral arrangements, prepaid funerals, and prearranged funerals?

A pre-need funeral contract involves a funeral purchased while the person is alive (and often while still well, too). It is a prepaid funeral by another name. According to AARP research, almost half of people who prepay funerals or burials pay in installments over time. The rest pay a lump sum. By contrast, a prearranged funeral is a funeral that is planned in advance, though payment is not made until the actual death. There are differing state laws governing how prepaid funerals should be handled. New York and New Jersey, for example, offer the most protection to consumers. Why do you need protection? Because all kinds of issues are involved. For example, the Funeral Consumers Alliance of Kansas City has found at least one-third of funerals involve prepayment, which is usually funded by insurance or through a trust, which may be revocable or irrevocable.

If you decide to prearrange or prepay for a funeral, be prepared to invest time and effort, and understand that emotions are also involved. For some of us, contemplating our own death is unpleasant enough—without adding daunting details. Yet others feel perfectly comfortable deciding on which flowers (and how many) to choose, investigating burial and/or cremation options, and planning (or eliminating) a visitation.

It's complicated, which is why some funeral industry experts advise against it. Buying a house and getting a mortgage is part of life for many of us, yet planning your death can feel like torture. It's an "I don't want to" scenario for some of us.

Key Questions and Considerations Before Signing a Pre-Need Funeral Contract:

- What if the funeral home closes down before you die?
- What if you move to another state? Can your contract be honored by another funeral home?
- Inflation is always an issue. If you live several years and prices for contracted services rise, does your family have to make up the difference?
- Does the contract contain any gotchas? Carefully review the contract to make sure there are no extra costs for "final expense funding."

95.

What should I know about cemetery plots?

Research shows a big drop in plot ownership among people aged forty and over. Only 34 percent own plots for themselves. Because fewer and fewer plots are available (cemeteries are filling up), there's no time to waste. Note that every cemetery has rules and regulations regarding size and nature of gravestones.

Where do you want to be buried?

Near already-deceased loved ones? Get started by calling cemeteries where relatives lie to get an idea of plot availability and costs. If you've heard about other cemeteries that sound appealing, check with them, too.

Do you want to buy one plot for yourself—or plots for your spouse and/or children, too?

Plots tend to be cheaper if you buy more than one. In addition, if family members lie near each other, it's easier for survivors to visit the graves. In one family I know, one son wanted a plot near his parents' plots; his brother wasn't ready to make the decision and opted out.

What's your price range?

Price has a lot to do with where you live. Expect much higher costs in the New York area and other big cities than, say, in a small Midwestern town. For example, two adjacent plots in one Dallas cemetery cost $7,000; two side-by-side plots in a New Jersey cemetery cost $2,300; and the cost per grave in a Chicago cemetery runs $1,900 to $6,000. At one cemetery in Minneapolis, a single adult grave starts at $2,350, not counting interment charges and myriad other costs. Private cemeteries tend to be more expensive than public ones. On the other hand, you can find bargains. There's a robust market for preowned plots. You can even find them on Ebay.com. Incidentally, a grave marker can run a few hundred dollars to thousands depending on size and material chosen.

Do you want a cemetery affiliated with a particular religion?

Some cemeteries are devoted exclusively to one religion; others offer different sections for a variety of denominations. This is an important consideration for many people. Do your homework. Good places to start include recommendations from your place of worship and/or family and friends.

96. What does it take to be buried at Arlington National Cemetery?

This is the country's premier cemetery for active duty military personnel and retired reservists, and recipients of the Medal of Honor and other high military decorations. Others buried in

Arlington include astronauts, US presidents and their families, Supreme Court Justices, and prominent figures in politics, sports, medicine, and other categories. Even three World War II prisoners of war (two Italians and one German) lie there, as the Geneva Convention required proper burial for them.

The first burial took place in 1864 on General Robert E. Lee's Virginia estate, which had been confiscated by the Union for the establishment of a new military cemetery. The remains of 2,111 unknown Civil War soldiers were interred there. Soldiers' remains from the Revolutionary War and the War of 1812 were later transferred there. Interestingly, there soon may no longer be any remains at the Tomb of the Unknowns, which was built after World War I, because remains can be identified today through DNA testing.

Currently, there are about twenty-five burials a day at Arlington. Due to space considerations, the Army is considering limiting future burials by excluding some personnel who are presently eligible. To check on your eligibility for Arlington, go to their website (arlingtoncemetery.mil).

Arlington and the United States Soldiers' & Airmen's Home National Cemetery are maintained by the Department of the Army. Soldiers from the 3rd US Infantry Regiment post flags in front of each grave every Memorial Day.

The Unique Traditions of Firefighter Funerals

It's customary to honor fallen firefighters and police officers. For example, when a New York State trooper was shot and killed in the line of duty, fellow troopers (some on horseback) saluted and honored him. The coffin was draped with the American flag. At a time when traditions in our society, which tend to anchor and support us, keep falling by the wayside, dissolving the "glue" of community, such funerals serve to remind us of the value of public service and camaraderie.

According to Stephen James Johnson, a fire company chaplain in a Connecticut fire company, a dead firefighter is family even if you don't know the deceased at all. Firemen cook, eat, and respond to calls together and are dedicated to public service. They die not just from fires but also explosions and other events.

Says Johnson, "We're a brotherhood and there's an instant system in place. It's all about the bereaved. The family is assigned a 'family officer' to ensure all goes smoothly at a funeral. A fireman guard stands at each end of the casket. You don't have to salute. They're there to make sure everything goes according to plan."

Firefighters are a true community, as are the military, the police, and EMTs. Comradeship and mutual caring for each other and each other's families are hallmarks. The codified system provides tangible help with programs and traditions in place that are ready to jump in at any moment.

"Death in a family is chaos, but here it's all worked out and ready 24/7. 'You are not alone,' has true meaning for families. We go to work every day with a chance of injury or death at any time," says Johnson.

97. How many other national cemeteries are there in the United States?

According to the Department of Veterans Affairs National Cemetery Administration, there are 135 national cemeteries in forty states (and Puerto Rico). Several states also maintain their own veterans cemeteries, but they may restrict eligibility to state residents. Burial at sea is possible through the United States Navy Mortuary Affairs Burial at Sea Program. Call 1-866-787-0081 for details. It's a toll free call.

Arlington isn't the only place that's getting crowded. So are many other cemeteries. There's only a finite amount of land available in places that can be reached by the general population. That's one of the reasons (aside from reducing costs) that cremation has overtaken burial.

Even London's 1,000-year-old Westminster Abbey has space issues. The Abbey is the final resting place for kings and queens of England, some of the world's greatest thinkers, poets, and scientists. Stephen Hawking's ashes were recently interred there, next to the remains of Charles Darwin and Isaac Newton.

98. What happens to bodies of the unclaimed dead today? Is there still a potter's field, and why was it named that way?

According to the Pennsylvania Historical and Museum Commission, "potter's field" was an American term that originally described land unfit for agriculture and only useful as clay for potters. A potter's field is ground reserved as a burial place for the poor, the friendless, and strangers. The graves are unmarked, and a potter's field can turn up in unexpected places. For example, Revolutionary War soldiers, victims of yellow fever, prison inmates, and slaves were buried in unmarked graves near Independence Hall in Philadelphia.

The Cook County Cemetery in Dunning, Illinois (a suburb of Chicago), was the final resting place for people under the care of many Cook County institutions, including the county's poor house, insane asylum, and consumptive hospital in the 1800s. It also became the potter's field for the poor and indigent of Chicago.

In New York City the unclaimed dead rest on Hart Island, which lies off the coast of the Bronx. People are buried en masse in trenches (not individual graves). During the AIDS epidemic in the 1980s and '90s, Hart Island was used as the final resting place for AIDS victims, who were buried in individual graves due to fear of contamination. This epidemic was treated like a plague. About 400,000 people died of AIDS in the United States during that period, 100,000 of them in New York City.

Today most cities in the United States cremate unclaimed bodies.

99. Should I write an obituary or epitaph for myself, and if so, how do I do it? What about a photo?

According to Legacy.com, less than 1 percent of obituaries it runs are written in advance by the deceased. Even so, more and more people are doing it. Some people distribute a draft of the obituary to friends and relatives for comments. One book about the process is *How to Write an Online Obituary: Virtual Memorials Made Simple* by Melissa Jayne Kinsey. The website Obituary Guide (obituaryguide.com) offers a template. Legacy.com offers a free tool called ObitWriter.

Writing your own obituary allows you to shape what you want to say and ensures the emphasis is where you want it. It's a gift to your survivors, too, who will be overwhelmed enough with the funeral and other details at the time of your death. Keep a draft of your obituary along with your other important documents.

Consider whether to choose a photo of yourself (now). You can also leave this up to your survivors. That said, selecting your own photo can relieve them of some stress, because it eliminates disagreement about which picture to choose (and whether to include one at all). You might leave instructions for how to handle a photo, and maybe attach the one you prefer (which can be updated periodically).

Obits often include photos of the deceased taken decades ago. There are any number of reasons for this. Maybe there's a need for the family to "see" the deceased as he was at his best. Or the deceased may have requested it. In obits that originate from the archives of newspapers, some photos include the date when the photograph was taken, as in, "Mary Thomas in 1981." For my obit, I personally hope my family will choose a flattering photo taken in recent years before my death.

An epitaph is a commemorative inscription on a gravestone. People use poetry, verses from the Bible, or their own words. It's important to think through your ideas and perhaps discuss them with those who are near and dear to you to get their "take." Remember, this is permanent. Do you want to mention your admirable qualities? One woman's preference for herself was, "She loved her children well."

100.

How do you leave your body to science, or donate your organs?

The federal government doesn't monitor statistics on whole body donations, but researchers estimate less than 20,000 bodies are donated annually. A Johns Hopkins study in 2004 found that about half of Americans would consider giving such a gift. In 2016, several American medical schools reported a spike in actual donations. The jump was attributed to soaring funeral prices and less religious stigma regarding the donation of remains. Major religions support organ donations or consider it a personal decision.

When it comes to organ donation, one organ donor can actually save up to eight people. One eye and tissue donor can save or improve the lives of up to fifty people, according to the Finger Lakes Donor Recovery Network. The kidney, heart, lungs, liver, small bowel, and pancreas are organs that may be transplanted. Usable tissue includes eyes, heart valves, bone, skin, veins, and tendons. Many people in their eighties and nineties have made successful donations. The Uniform Anatomical Gift Act governs organ donation and anatomical gifts of cadavers for medical education and research. We often hear of donations of a kidney or a heart, but whole body donations are rarer—although they are in demand by the nation's almost 140 medical schools to train doctors. Donation is a real service to humanity and helps to maintain and improve medical care for all of us. Not every body is accepted, however. Perhaps

10 percent are turned down, often because the cadaver is too large or overweight for equipment to handle. Contact a medical school in your area for detailed information on donation programs.

Nonprofit organ procurement organizations have been created by Congress to coordinate and promote donations throughout the country, but their donation rates vary widely. According to the US Department of Health & Human Services, there is no age limit to donate. What counts is your medical condition. This criteria will be used when deciding which of your organs and tissues are eligible for transplant or medical research. In 2017, over 61 percent of organ recipients were aged fifty and over; more than 19 percent were aged sixty-five or older. For more information, see the website for the US Government Information on Organ Donation and Transplantation (organdonor.gov).

There are 138 million donor registrations in the United States. According to the United Network for Organ Sharing (UNOS), the overwhelming majority of Americans support organ donation, but only 54 percent are registered donors.

Exhumation

To exhume is to remove a body or cremated remains from its resting place. The word *exhume* derives from the Latin and means "out of earth." States and localities regulate the process of exhumation.

Crime novels, movies, and TV series have all featured exhumations as plot details such as rechecking a cause of death and aiding a criminal investigation. But the process sometimes turns up in the news, as well. A recent controversy surrounds the proposed exhumation of Spain's fascist dictator Francisco Franco, who won the Spanish Civil War in 1939. Franco was buried near Madrid in a basilica that took almost two decades to build. Why dig him up? To transfer Franco's embalmed body to a less opulent resting place.

Another reason to exhume: to confirm the identity of a body or cremated remains. In 1998 the remains of a soldier who died in the Vietnam War were removed from the Tomb of the Unknown Soldier in Arlington National Cemetery for DNA testing. Exhumation also may be done to obtain DNA to identify the dead in natural disasters or mass calamities.

101.

What is an advance directive? Does it ensure my interests are protected when I am physically or mentally incapable of making life and death decisions?

An advance directive is a written statement of your wishes if you are dying and are unable to make judgments about medical treatment on your own, such as in cases of cerebral hemorrhage or massive stroke or grave injury.

Preparing to die, whether soon—or decades from now—is complicated, yet oh so necessary if you want to save yourself or your loved ones from unnecessary grief. None of us want to plan for death—ours or someone else's. And it used to be a simple matter. Seventy years ago, we died in our own beds at home. What went on was between the doctor, patient, and family. But that was then. Today, it can seem like you need to go to law school to arrange the kind of death you want in the event you are incapacitated. The issues, decisions, and stress can overwhelm the calmest among us. An advance directive is designed to speak for you when you can't. It asks that you consider your options ahead of a crisis.

What do you want to happen if you can no longer breathe on your own? Do you want to spend whatever time is left hooked up to a machine? If you've had a massive coronary that has destroyed your heart and there is no hope, do you want CPR the next time? How do you feel about a feeding tube if it will only prolong a horrible dying process? If a doctor says the next step for your care means going into intensive care with virtually no chance of leaving it, do you really want that? Or do you want to go somewhere else, perhaps hospice?

It's enormously comforting to have a document you've signed that specifies what measures you want taken, or not taken. I've gone through the process of following an advance directive myself when two of my closest loved ones died. I felt as if I was sleepwalking. Yet it was an enormous relief to have the patient's own wishes to guide me.

It's advisable to check your advance directive and other related documents every five years or so to ensure that, if your situation and your own feelings have changed in any way, you can make necessary adjustments on paper. Other advance directives include a health care proxy, a do not resuscitate order, and an organ donation form. A living will is another type of advance directive. It's a statement of your desires regarding medical treatment if you are unable to express informed consent yourself.

Hospices and Palliative Care

Hospice is end-of-life care. It can be provided at home, in a nursing home, assisted living facility, inpatient hospital, or hospice facility. Anyone seriously ill with only a short time to live can be treated in hospice. Symptoms will be relieved as much as possible, if desired. However, hospice will not provide curative treatment. Hospice is a benefit provided to individuals who are eligible for Medicare Part A (hospital insurance) and certified as terminally ill by a physician. The patient must have a prognosis of six months or less to live. If the person lives longer (and the doctor certifies that death remains close), Medicare services can continue.

Medicare's hospice benefit offers four levels of care: (1) Routine care, the most common, provides care at home; (2) General inpatient care offers pain control and other symptom management not available at home; (3) Continuous home care. The latter provides care from between eight to twenty-four hours a day, and must consist mostly of nursing care plus caregiver and hospice services. (4) Inpatient respite care gives the primary caregiver a rest when needed. During this time, the patient stays in a hospital, long-term care facility with appropriate nursing, or a hospice care facility for up to five consecutive days. Hospice also includes counseling or grief support for both patients and their loved ones. Hospice requires volunteers to provide a minimum of 5 percent of total hours of care.

Some private insurance plans cover hospice, as well. Length and type of care varies depending on the plan and situation.

In 2016 (the latest figures available), 27.9 percent of Medicare patients in hospice received one to seven days of care, and 74.5 percent received one to ninety days of care, according to the National Hospice and Palliative Care Organization.

Palliative care treats anyone with a serious illness and allows for the continuation of curative treatment. Medicare might pay for it, depending on the benefits and treatment plan of the insured. Private insurance coverage depends on the plan.

102. How is a POLST (Physician Orders for Life Sustaining Treatment) different from an advance directive?

POLST is an approach to end-of-life planning that helps elicit, document, and honor patient treatment wishes. Although an advance directive is appropriate for healthy patients, a POLST is for seriously ill or frail patients who are at risk for a major medical crisis within the next year. It emphasizes advance care planning conversations among patients, doctors, and family members; and shared decision-making between a patient and health care professionals about the patient's treatment wishes regarding extreme lifesaving measures. You can find POLST forms and organ donation registries online at Everplans (ever plans.com). Look for their State-by-State Guides.

A 2014 study in the *Journal of the American Geriatrics Society* found patients who filled out a POLST form to request things like a "Do not resuscitate" order or a "Comfort measures only" order were far less likely to die in a hospital. Most states have adopted POLST or are developing programs like it.

103.

My mother is in hospice and hasn't long to live. I'm executor of her will and know there are certain documents I will need to handle her finances and other issues. What are they?

You will need certified copies of the death certificate, which you can get by contacting the health department of the locality in which your mother dies. You can usually order them online or by phone or mail. Be prepared: They're expensive, as much as $30 a copy, depending on locality. If you use a funeral home when the time comes, you may be able to get a few copies of the death certificate without charge.

Letters testamentary (also known as letters of administration) are documents, issued by the probate court to the executor of the estate, authorizing the executor to settle the estate according to terms of the will. You might need to have certified copies of the letters to deal with the deceased's bank, broker, or government agencies.

You will also need the will, insurance policies, tax returns, and more. Many people hire an attorney who specializes in wills, trusts, and estates to help them through the quagmire.

104. Is there such a thing as funerals for pets these days?

As a matter of fact there is. We've all heard of pet cemeteries, so why be astonished by funerals, as well? To their owners, pets can be considered people. If you have a pet, you know what to say to a bereaved owner. If you don't, it may be hard to comprehend the grief felt by someone who lived with an animal for years. In fact, the great British poet Lord Byron wrote the poem "Epitaph to a Dog" to commemorate Boatswain, his Newfoundland dog, who died of rabies in 1808. The poem is inscribed on the dog's tomb, which is actually larger than the tomb of Byron himself.

In Thailand and other Buddhist countries, funerals for dogs and other pets (including snakes, turtles, and other creatures) are routine. Buddhists believe in an afterlife for animals. Even a goldfish can be cremated at a temple, prayed over by monks, and readied for reincarnation. A pet's ashes may be scattered in a river or other body of water or kept in an urn at home. Nirvana is for animals, too, and monks pray for the latter in temples. Funerals help them transition into a new life.

Here in the United States, there are funeral homes specifically for pets, which will also provide caskets or urns if desired. According to the National Funeral Directors Association, 17.2 percent of funeral homes in the United States will cremate your pet. In addition, another 13 percent expect to do so in the next few years. Some traditional funeral homes will also accommodate pet funerals if asked. Cities and counties usually have their own regulations, however.

Pet cremation has grown wildly popular for the same reasons the rates for the cremation of human bodies has skyrocketed. The price is right; it's clean; it's easy. Note that pets may be cremated communally unless you ask for individual cremation. There may also be mass burials of animals (cremated or not). Some pets must be euthanized, which is another traumatic decision for the owner. The Association for Pet Loss and Bereavement (aplb.org) is a nonprofit that offers chat rooms and state-by-state listings of Pet Cemeteries and Cremations. Another resource is The Association for the Prevention of Cruelty to Animals. The International Association for Animal Hospice and Palliative Care (IAAHPC) provides support for pet owners and comfort care for animals with chronic and/ or life limiting diseases.

Some pet owners want the ashes of their pets placed in their own casket when they die. It's a good idea to check with both the funeral home and cemetery in advance to be sure that state law and cemetery policies allow for it.

Talking about Death and Grief

105. I've heard about bereavement groups and wonder if they truly help people who are grieving a death?

Research results on the effectiveness of bereavement groups are mixed. I personally attended a bereavement group after my husband died several years ago. I found it helpful in some ways and not in others. However, I was glad I had access to a group of people (mostly women, but a few men) who were also mourning spouses, as opposed to other relationships. The group was led by a social worker and a clergyman. Although the ages of group members varied, we shared so many of the same issues and after-effects. That would not have been the case if some members had lost parents or siblings or children. The group was particularly helpful with practical problems, such as whether to stop wearing a wedding ring, and when to do it (or not); how to deal with all the paperwork involved with finances, changing ownership of the car(s); and other thorny issues.

The once-a-week session gave structure to my life and "anchored" me in a way. And after the formal sessions ended, I and other group members decided to continue on our own and meet at local restaurants, without a group leader. I also learned practical tips on problems such as how to deal with my husband's business partners and when and how to clean out my mate's closet—and where to dispose of his belongings. I found some others in the group were having a much harder time than I was. I'm glad I had the group experience.

Overall, I felt it was important to have a professional leader of the group to make sure that false information could be corrected, and to curb people who might (consciously or not) dominate the group and take more than a fair share of the time allotted.

106. What is a Death Cafe and how does it work?

Death Cafes are a phenomenon that attract people of all ages who want to share conversations about grief and death. People are talking about death in new ways, and since the early 2000s, Death Cafes have been sweeping countries throughout Europe, South America, Australia, parts of Asia and Africa, as well as the United States. Suddenly the topic of death, which has been "hush-hush" in our society—people don't die; they pass away—is now out in the open. Death Cafes are led by a volunteer facilitator who may or may not be a social worker, grief counselor, hospice professional, or chaplain. The object is to talk about death in general, a particular death, loss, and other related subjects. Death Cafes are not "therapy" but venues for philosophical discussion, which has been common in Europe for centuries.

According to the Death Cafe website (deathcafe.com), there are 3,569 Death Cafes in the United States and 6,870 in a long list of other countries from Afghanistan and Bulgaria to Nigeria, Russia, and the United Kingdom. The first one in the United States took place in Ohio in 2012.

Death Cafes are especially popular with women, although men attend, as well, and they appeal to the under-thirty-five age group, as well as the over-sixty-five crowd. Attendees may be theists, believers in reincarnation, or observant in major religions. Death Cafes are nonprofit and participants must agree to keep the proceedings confidential. Stay home unless you agree to listen objectively to others religious views, and if you attend, refrain from pushing your own beliefs. The goal is to exchange information, not convert others to your point of view. For some it's a way to face up to fears and accept death (ours and other peoples), and live a fuller life.

Tea and cake are served as a bow to the nourishment of life.

107.
I get very upset and want to call mutual friends when I see the obituary of someone I know—a contemporary. Why is that?

You know you're getting older not only when you start reading obituaries but also when the deceased you read about are in your age group. At such times there are any number of reasons why we have a need to connect with others who knew the person. Ultimately, we feel threatened because any death is an unwelcome reminder of our own mortality. The deaths of our contemporaries make us wonder deep down, "Will I be next?"

Reaching out also helps us heal. We want to confirm and illuminate what we know about the deceased—to share memories and compare experiences with someone who understands. Why? Because we're social animals created and designed to help each other grieve. It may be easier to mourn alone, but we do better when we mourn in a community. We process the loss better. It's no accident that people congregate to grieve together in every religion. Talking with mutual friends of the deceased helps us make sense of our own experiences and impressions. These conversations help provide a more complete picture of the deceased's impact on our lives.

In cases of tragedy, we want to share our recollections as well as our sorrows. A mutual friend can remember with us. Compare that experience with talking to someone who knows nothing about the deceased. For one thing, you would have to fill in a lot of background information, which is unnecessary in the case of a mutual friend.

And it's not just the positive people you want to talk about. One obituary that stopped me in my tracks announced the death of a business associate I knew years ago. My memories were negative—he was a nasty man—but I still wanted to discuss him with someone else who knew him and perhaps hear another perspective. Maybe we want to find the "good," even if the person caused us misery.

Today, technology offers new ways to congregate and grieve a death together. Research published in 2017 in the journal *Nature Human Behavior* measured recovery and resilience after the death of a mutual friend on 15,000 Facebook networks. Interactions among people grieving the loss increased 30 percent, and the ties continued for years. The eighteen to twenty-four age group experienced the best recovery.

108. How do you talk to someone in hospice?

Who wants to visit someone who is dying? Raise your hand. Unless you're a chaplain, a social worker, or an unusually understanding person, you're likely to feel awkward at best, intimidated, or even terrified of the encounter. What do you say? What if the person starts crying hysterically or says, "I don't want to live anymore?" How do you respond? What should you expect?

Most of us are terrified by the prospect of death—and we assume the patient feels the same. But research by Kurt Gray, an associate professor of psychology at the University of North Carolina at Chapel Hill, and his coauthors found out otherwise. They analyzed blog posts of people terminally ill with either cancer or ALS—and compared them with the posts of a perfectly healthy online group that was asked to imagine they were terminal. The results were surprising. Terminally ill patients were thinking about meaning and used more positive words, such as "happiness" and "love," and fewer emotionally negative words like "fear," "terror," and "anxiety."

When visiting someone in hospice, it helps to know that the person is well aware that death awaits, whether hospice services take place at home, in an independent hospice setting, or in the hospital. Hospice patients have six months or less to live, although some live longer. This is a time for both gentleness and emotional honesty—traits that can be in short supply. Before you visit, think about what you might want to discuss with the person. I've said: "How are you managing?"; "How are they treating you?"; and "Tell me how this hospice works." If the person is in a wheelchair, ask if they'd like to go outdoors (weather permitting). But be honest with yourself. If you don't want to go, don't force it. You might find yourself in an awkward situation that benefits no one. Call or write instead.

When you visit, what should you do if the person says, "I don't want to live anymore"? Don't deny the statement with, "Oh, you don't really mean that." Instead, try "Tell me about it." Or echo the words, as in, "So that's how you feel."

Note that usually the person will not be upset, although we fear that. (What will we do then?) To avoid uncomfortable silences, come prepared to ask questions about the person's interests or expertise, as in, "You know I wanted to make lasagna last week but forgot how much basil to add to your recipe."

I spoke to two people before they died, and I did a good job on one. I wish I'd thought out the other visit beforehand—and yes, even wrote a script. I might not have followed it exactly, but I'd have known what I wanted to express and why. It's about saying good-bye without saying good-bye. Something as simple as "I love you" can do the trick.

A minister once told me, "It's easier to deal with a sudden death. Hospice is like a really long wake."

Note that hospice also includes counseling or grief support for both patients and their loved ones.

Visiting the Dying

- Make arrangements in advance and find out how long you can plan to stay.
- Think before you go. Rehearse conversation starters like "How is today?"
- Greet the person as you usually do—with a hug or kiss, a handshake, or "I miss you" or "The office (or tennis) isn't the same without you."
- Let the patient lead the conversation.
- Talk about shared memories like the cruise you took together or the hitchhiking trip in Europe during a college break. There's nothing like "old times" to make both of you "come alive."
- Ask, "Is there anything that gives you comfort now?"
- Tell how much impact your friendship with the person has made on your life.
- Bring a photo album of good times, or bring music or a book if the person is likely to be able to enjoy it.
- Do not talk about religion unless you know the person has one. It's too easy to say something inappropriate. Avoid references to God and heaven unless you are positive you know the patient's beliefs.
- Talk about what's going on in the world. People know what the future holds—but there is "now," too. Sports can be a good conversation topic for a football, baseball, or soccer fan.

109. What's a "death doula"?

To most of us, a doula is someone who helps a woman giving birth. However, now there's another kind, a so-called death doula. These doulas can complement hospice services through comforting rituals that help the dying person talk and reflect on life's meaning—and also inform the family of what to expect. They can help the family plan the final days.

End of life doulas focus on "a good death," which includes caring for the emotional needs of the patient. Care and support systems can change as patients move to a hospice facility—or possibly leave a hospice facility to die at home. A doula can move along with them from one setting to another. Medicare now pays for only the medical parts of doula services. Individual "packages" are by the hour. An end-of-life vigil may run from $1,500 to $3,500.

Volunteer death doulas who are trained to help people with limited family, or provide other support free of charge, are also available in some areas. The volunteers receive eight hours of training and must be comfortable with the idea of dying and death. Volunteers are matched with patients and are supervised. The International End of Life Doula Association (INELDA) was founded in 2015. Among other things, the association trains hospital staff members, including hospice personnel.

110. How can the loss of a friend differ from losing a family member?

Friendship often isn't accorded the same respect as other relationships in our society. Have you ever seen a friend listed as a survivor in an obituary? I've seen it just once. (It's so rare, I made a note of it!) So the death of a friend is often sidelined. Yet the loss can be a tremendous blow to the survivor, especially in these days of later marriage, divorce, and the aging population. Women are likelier to survive, and the loss of a dear friend can leave a chasm in one's life. Research shows a diversity of relationships and having many roles in life is good for our health and longevity. Friends choose each other, as opposed to relatives. Friends offer emotional support, help you cope with health issues, and/or share or introduce you to satisfying social and learning experiences. They are crucial to go on living a meaningful life after others have died.

Canadian research reveals young men react differently from women to the loss of a male friend. Men responded with emptiness, anger, stoicism, and sentimentality to deaths caused by auto accidents, adventure sports, drug overdose, and fights. Another study found men used binge drinking after the tragic death of a male friend as a way to express emotion, connect with others, and dull pain and sadness. Women have less problem crying and seeking support. Many men feel tears are not masculine, though hopefully that attitude is changing.

111. I've heard that some bereaved hallucinate about their deceased loved ones. Is it true?

Researchers at the University of Milan in Italy, after examining previous peer-reviewed research, did indeed find evidence of a high prevalence of post-bereavement hallucinatory experience (PBHE). They reported that 30 percent to 60 percent of widowed subjects who did not suffer from mental disorders had hallucinatory experiences such as seeing or hearing the deceased spouse. In addition, I know of one widow who talks occasionally to the picture of her late husband at times of joy or stress. Another widow, when her husband died in his thirties, raged at him in the shower for leaving her to deal with his irascible mother all alone.

112. What are "grief therapy" dogs? I've heard they're actually used at funerals. How does this work?

Certified therapy dogs are now being used at many funeral homes to help comfort families. Dogs are especially helpful for children who are grieving a loved one. According to the National Funeral Directors Association, canine use is on the rise to help reduce stress and anxiety among the bereaved—feelings that affect virtually everyone attending a funeral. Grief therapy dogs are mood changers and offer support.

·CONCLUSION·

As attitudes toward death, demographics, and a lengthening life span continue to evolve in our society, it's hard to predict what's in store. The National Funeral Directors Association (NFDA) conducts an annual consumer study. The results from their 2018 study found only 17.5 percent of people aged forty and over want to be buried. And of the 60.6 percent of those who want to be cremated, only 12.2 percent want a full funeral service with a viewing and visitation, preceding cremation.

As our society becomes less religious, we need all the support we can muster. What remains unshakable is the human need to assemble and comfort each other at times of loss. Will more of us share our fears of death with each other? Will new traditions emerge—and will they have the power of old ones? Through the centuries, rituals have sustained us and helped us continue on.

More changes are likely to occur in the future. For example, an NFDA spokesperson notes that new funeral homes being built are different from existing ones. In the future they might not even be called funeral homes. What then? "Funeral, cremation, and life tribute centers," he says. Newer homes will have a big room (nothing like a chapel). Those rooms will be used for weddings and birthday parties when not hosting funerals, which may or may not be traditional.

Thinking about the end of life brings up big issues and emotions. It's never too late to reach out and attempt to heal rifts (although it may demand a suspension of who's right and who's wrong). In my own family, the way it was done was to leave the past where it belongs: behind us. We learned to look forward, realizing that family is all we have. It is precious and must be protected. We learned to overlook at times, and to forgive at times, to hold our tongues and always ask, "Is it worth it to have this argument?" That doesn't mean we never disagree. The task is to agree to disagree and move some subjects off the table. Hopefully these pages have brought you closer to your own honest feelings about your loved ones who are still alive.

•ACKNOWLEDGMENTS•

This book would not have been possible without my agent, Linda Konner, who conceived of the concept originally. Linda has believed in and supported me through the years. Every writer should have a "Linda."

Andrew Isaacs and Jonathan and Katie Isaacs have been sounding boards and cheerleaders—always there when I need them.

I also thank a new friend, Beverly Nadler, who knows all about loss, and two old ones: Elaine Nathan, whose ideas and energy were extremely helpful, and Martha Halperin, who has always been there for me with her humanity and wisdom.

I'm so lucky to have all of you.

•INDEX•